MW01620854

I'm Lucy

A Day in the Life of a Young Bonobo

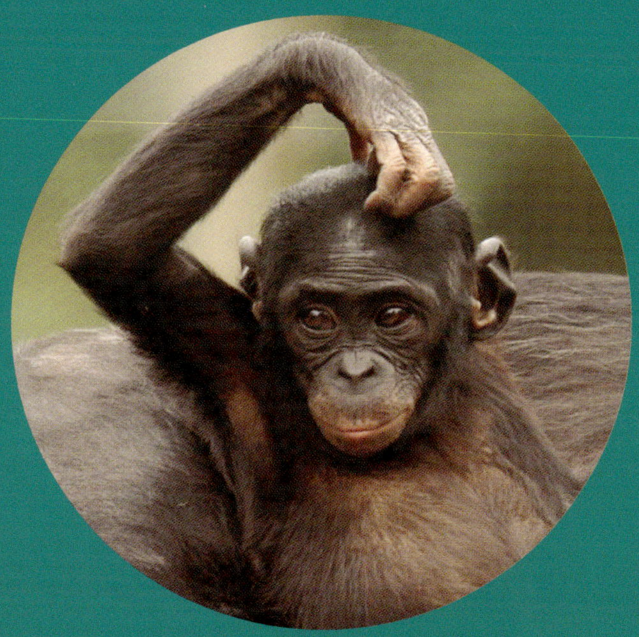

Written by Mathea Levine • Photographs by Marian Brickner

Afterword by Jane Goodall

BLUE BARK PRESS

This book is fondly dedicated to Ursula Goodenough whose generosity, love and true desire to help bonobos made this book a reality for us all. —M.L. and M.B.

For Isabella and Delilah, of course. —M.L.

To my children and grandchildren and Martin to whom I am eternally grateful. —M.B.

www.bonobokids.org

secret password: LIANA

Book design by Leslie Tane Design

Library of Congress Control Number: 2007943007
ISBN: 978-0-615-18110-3

First Printing

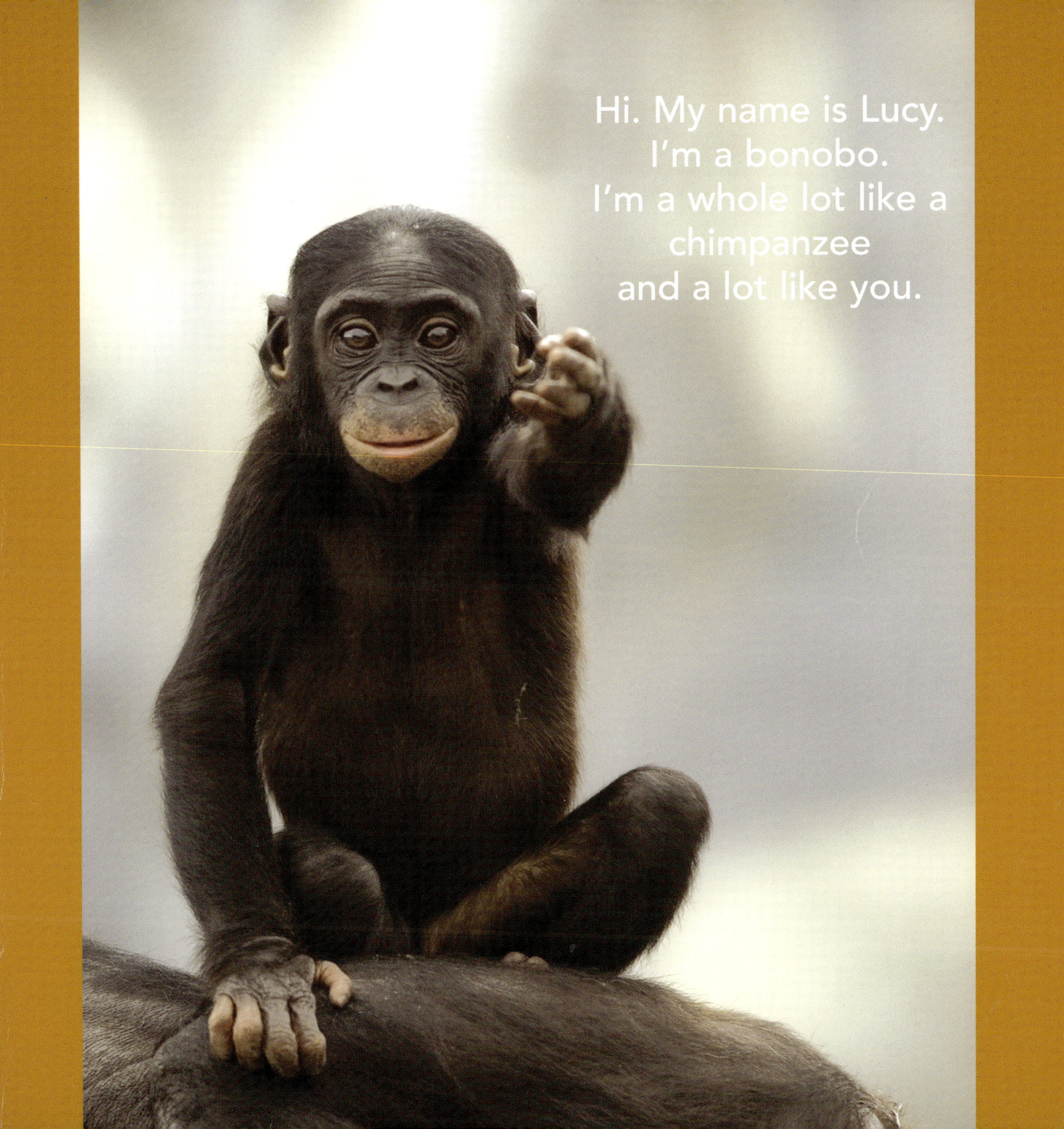

Hi. My name is Lucy.
I'm a bonobo.
I'm a whole lot like a
chimpanzee
and a lot like you.

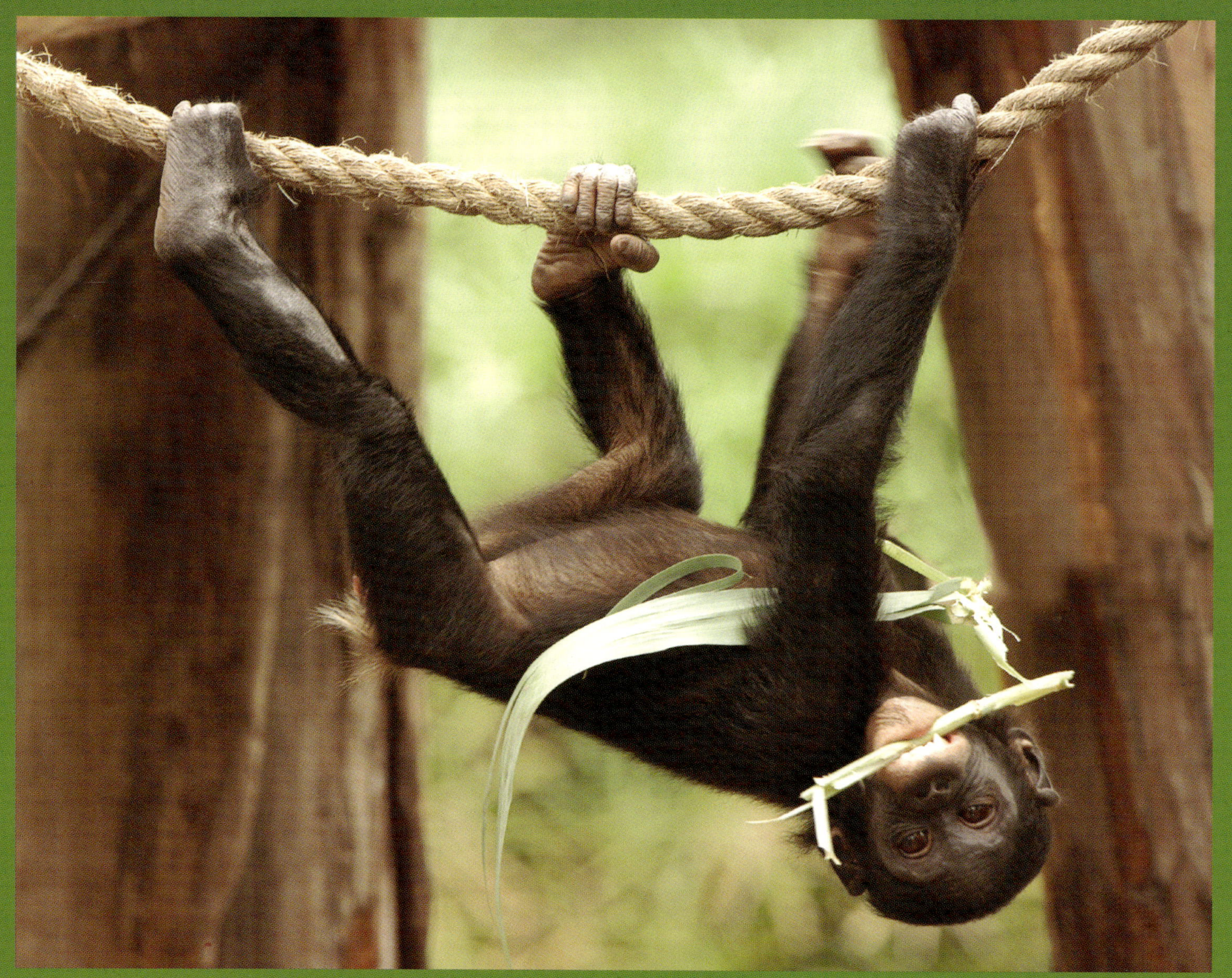

Bonobos come from a country in Africa called the Democratic Republic of Congo, but I live with my family at the zoo in Jacksonville, Florida.
I am almost two years old.
Here's what I look like upside down.

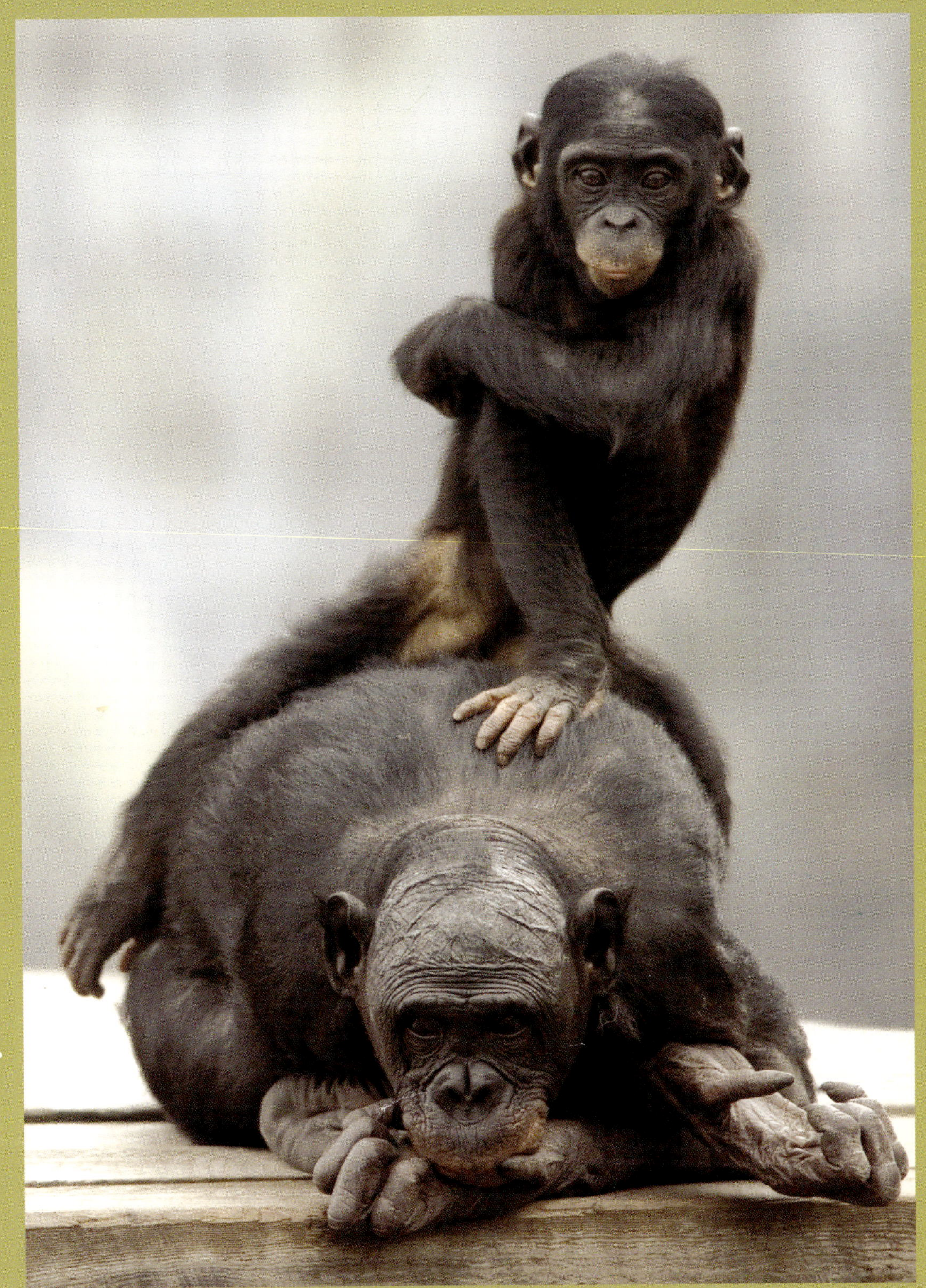

This is my mom. Her name is Lorel. Her back makes a really great chair.

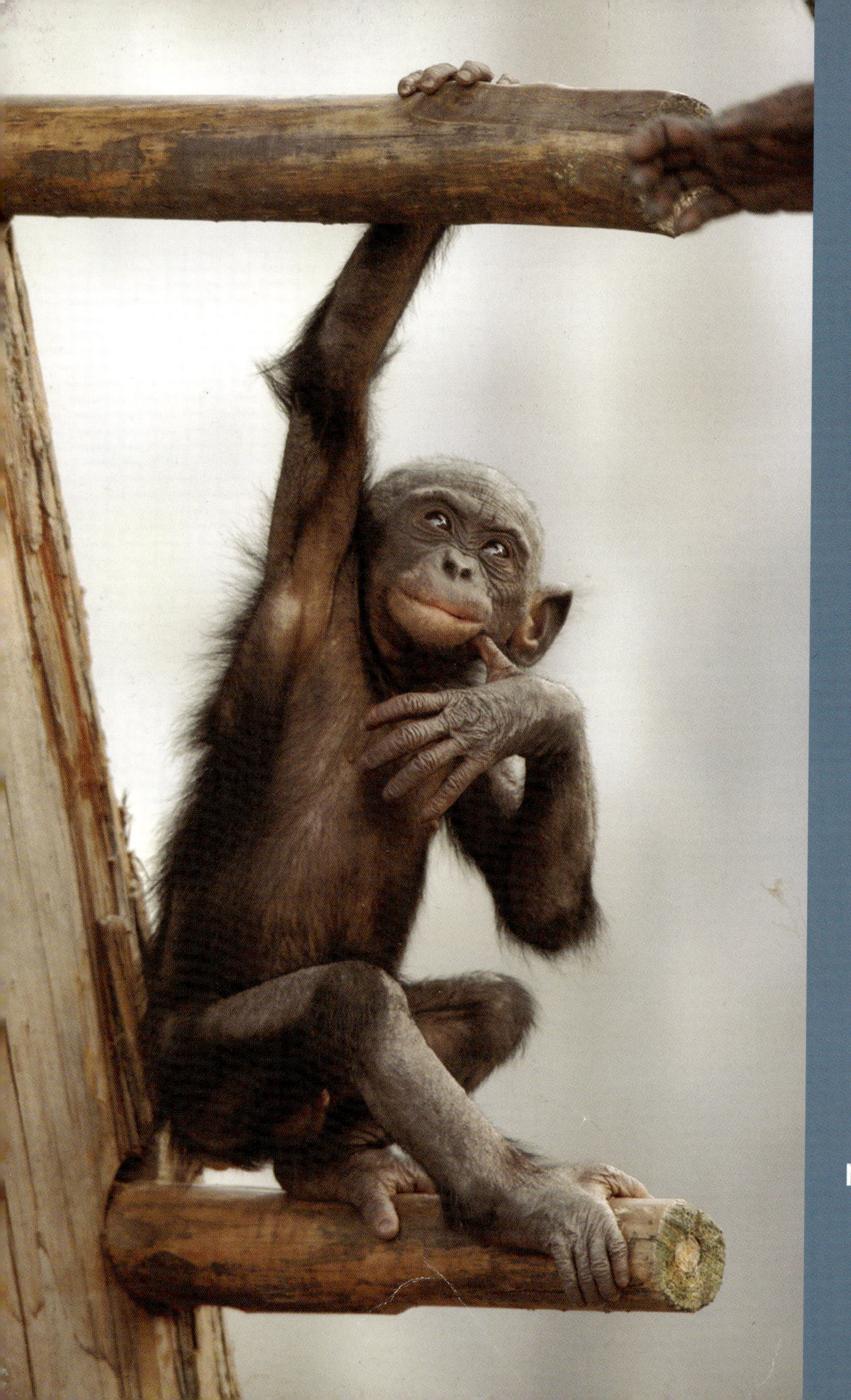

This is Kaleb. He is my little half brother. He has big ears and funny hair.

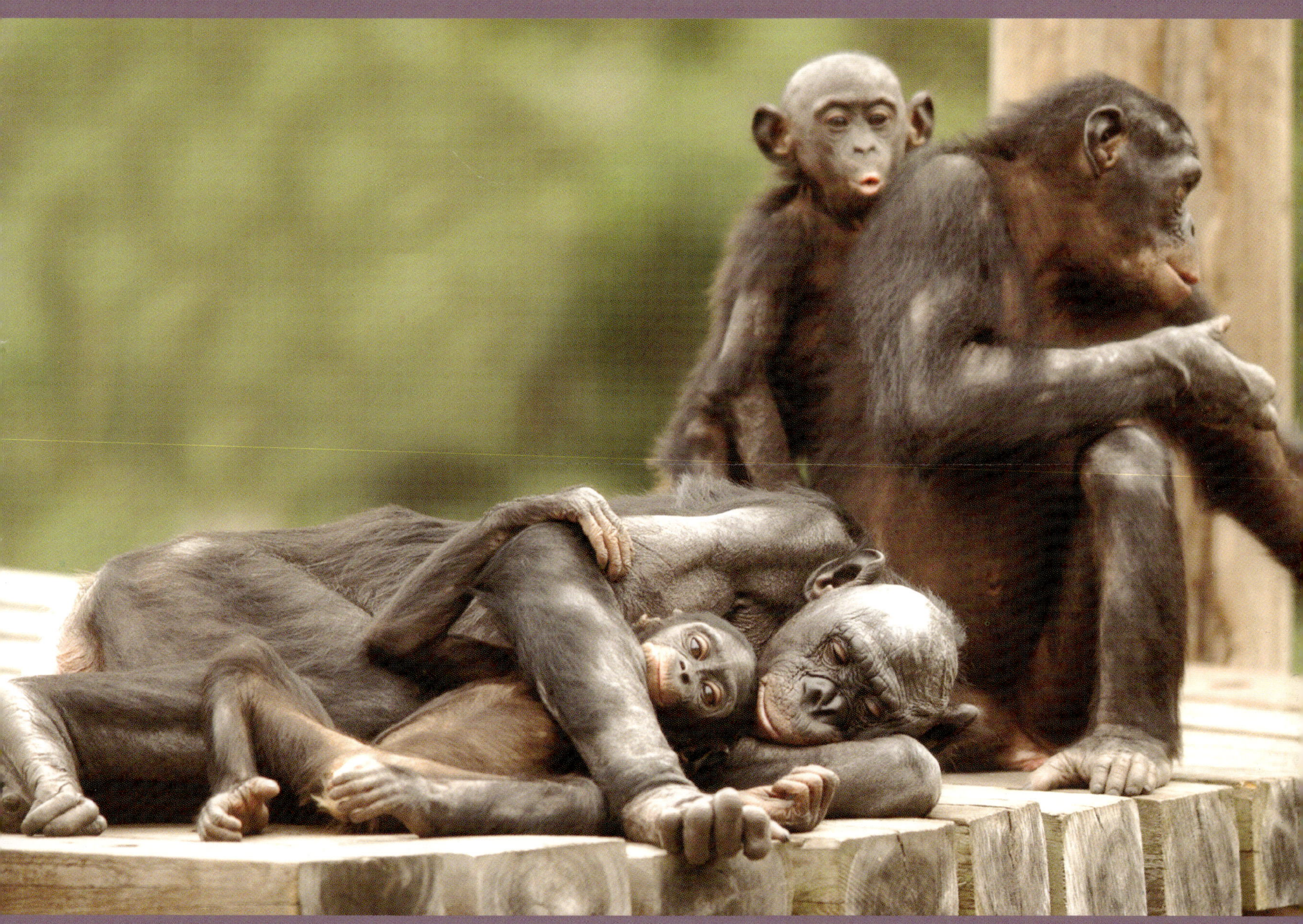

My Aunt Lexi lives with us too.
That's her on the right with Kaleb.
We all love each other very much.

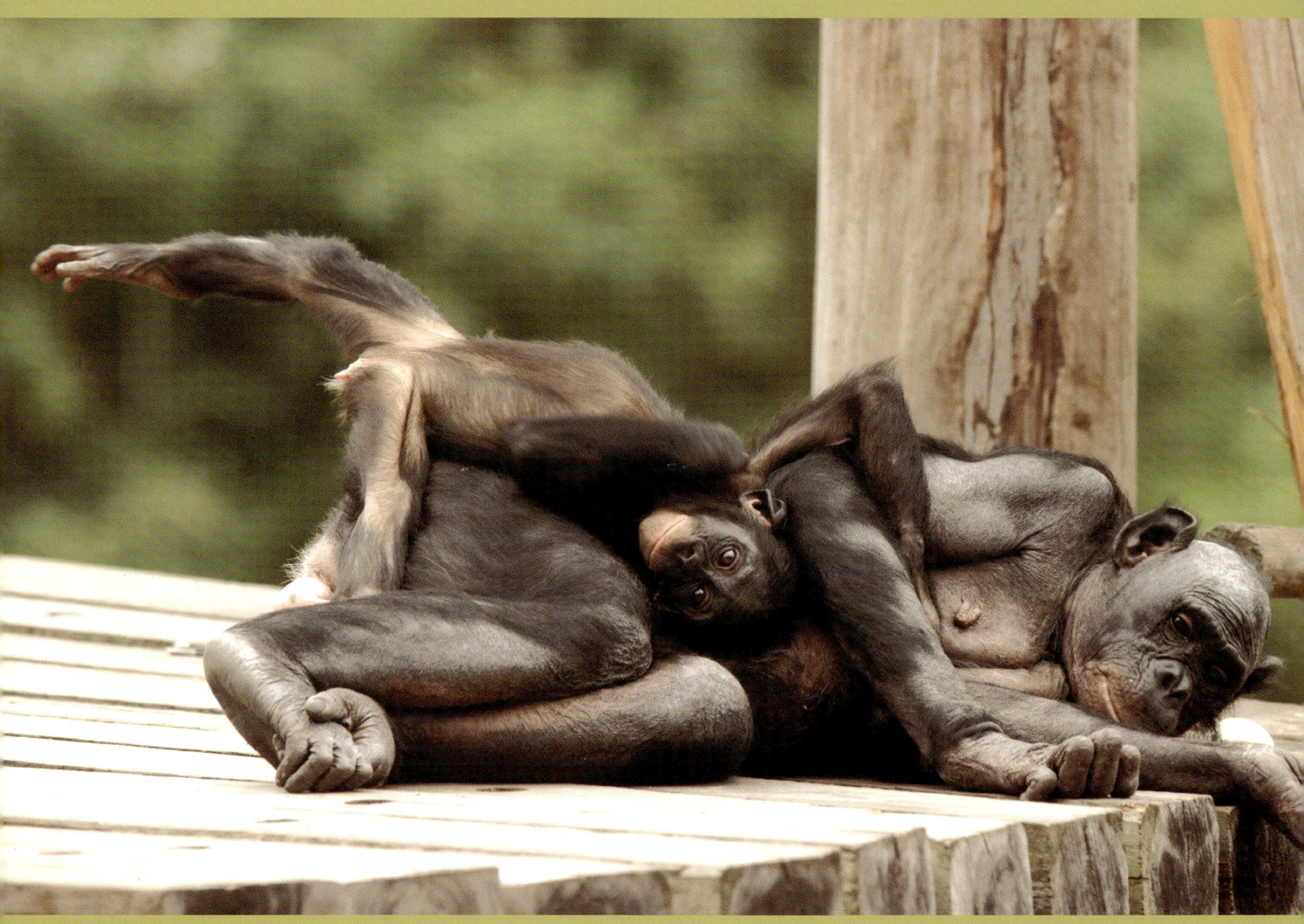

Since I'm still little, I spend a lot of time hanging out with my mom.

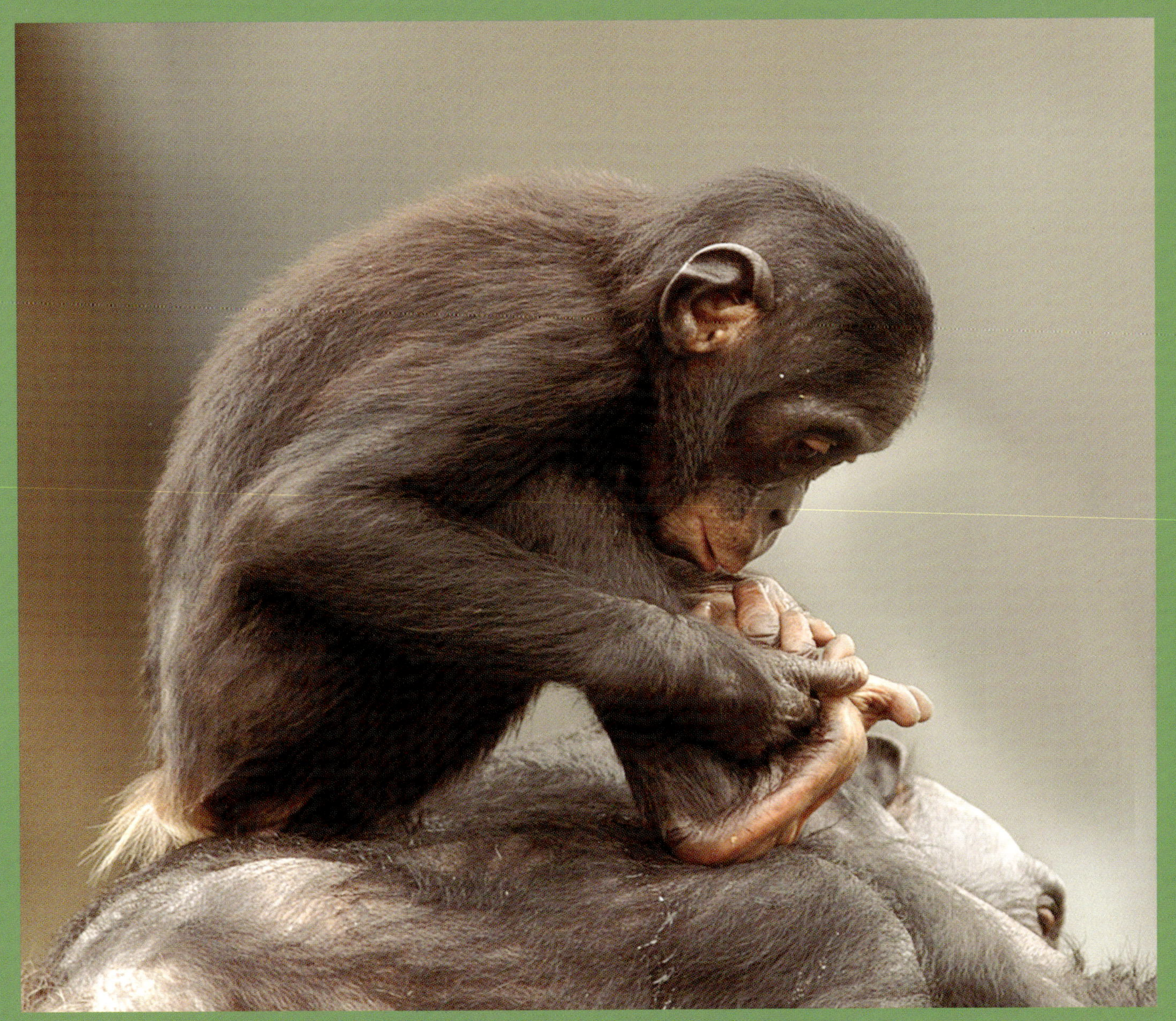

When this gets boring, I play with my toes.

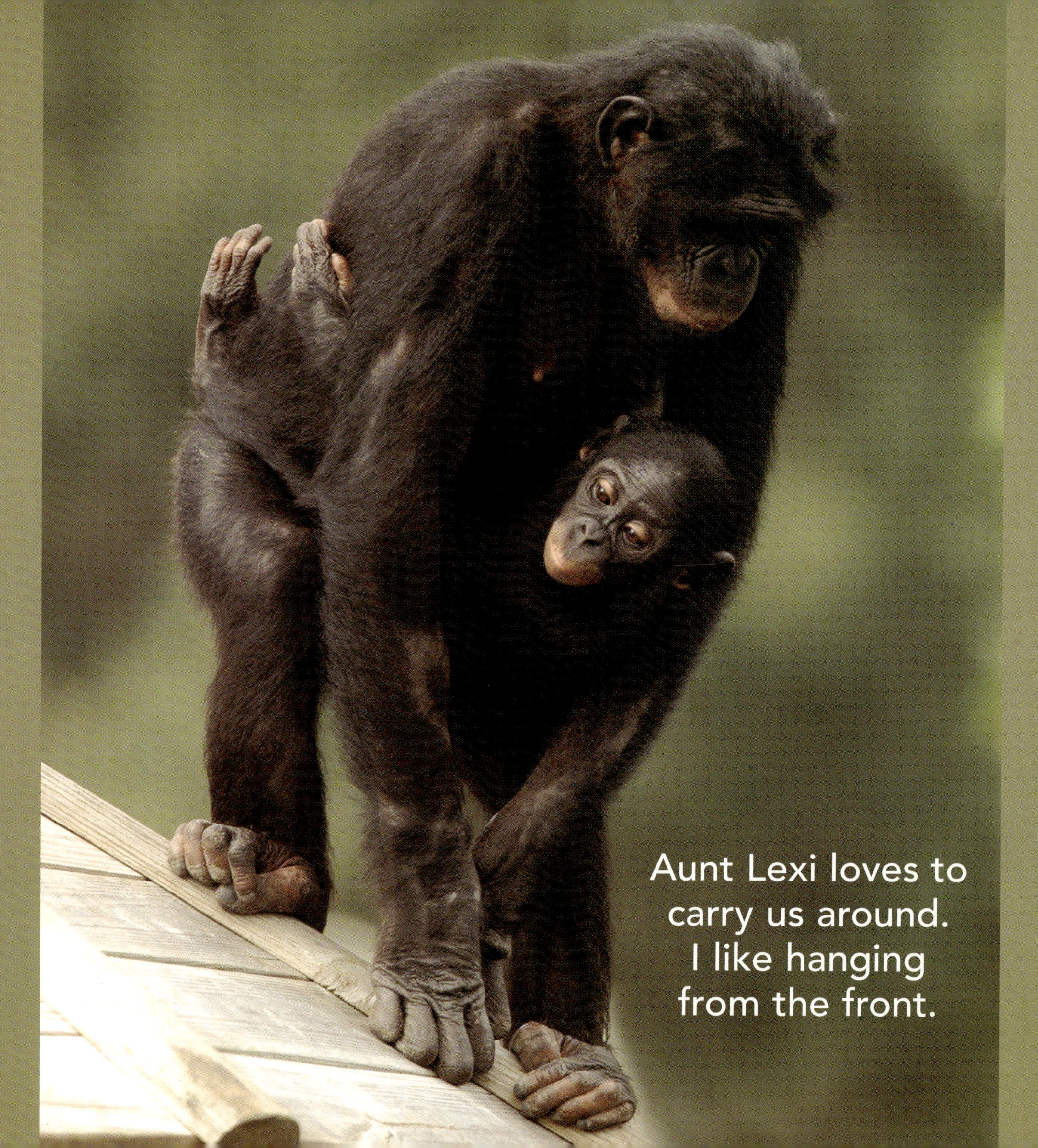

Aunt Lexi loves to
carry us around.
I like hanging
from the front.

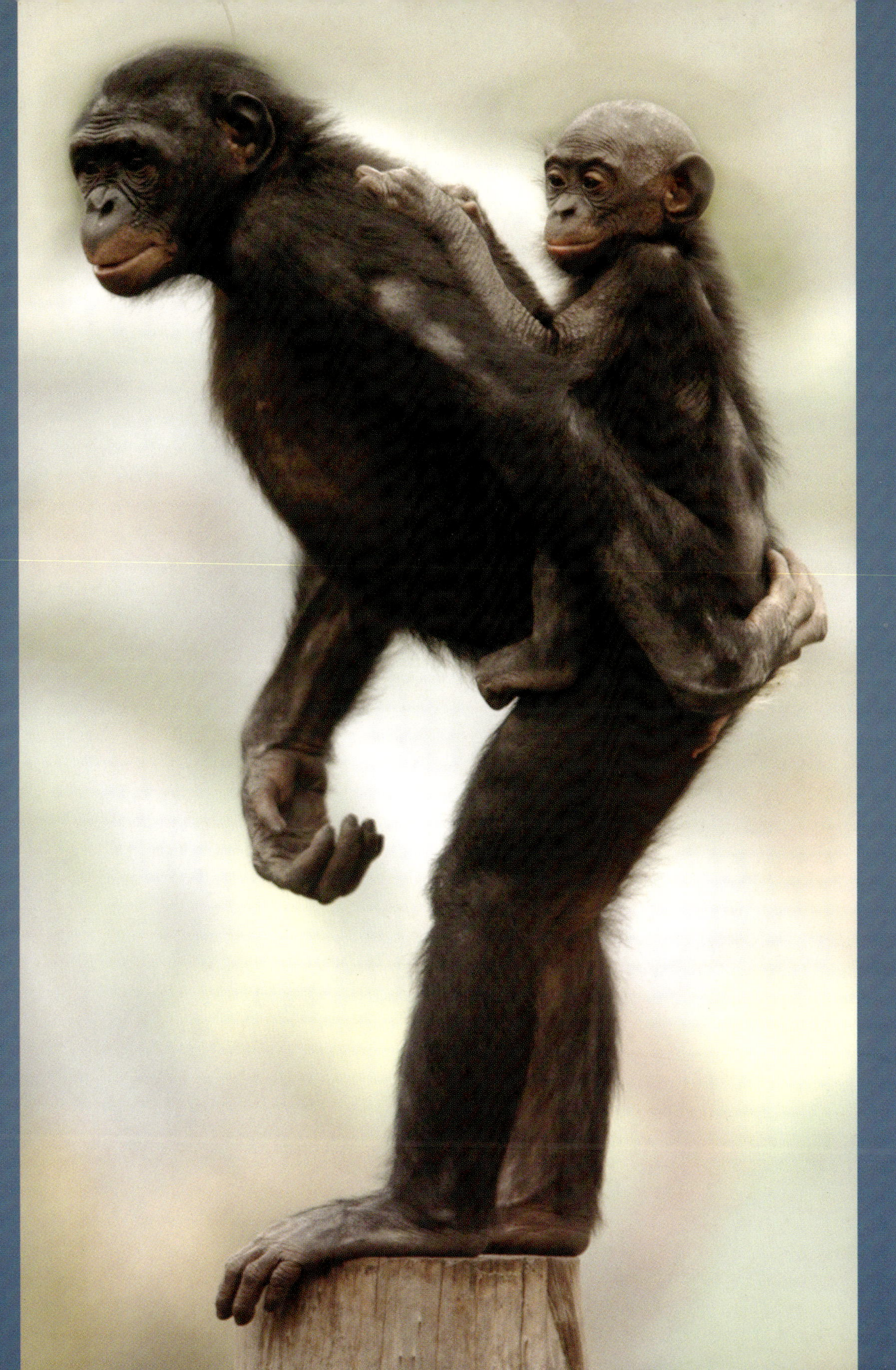

Kaleb likes
piggyback rides.

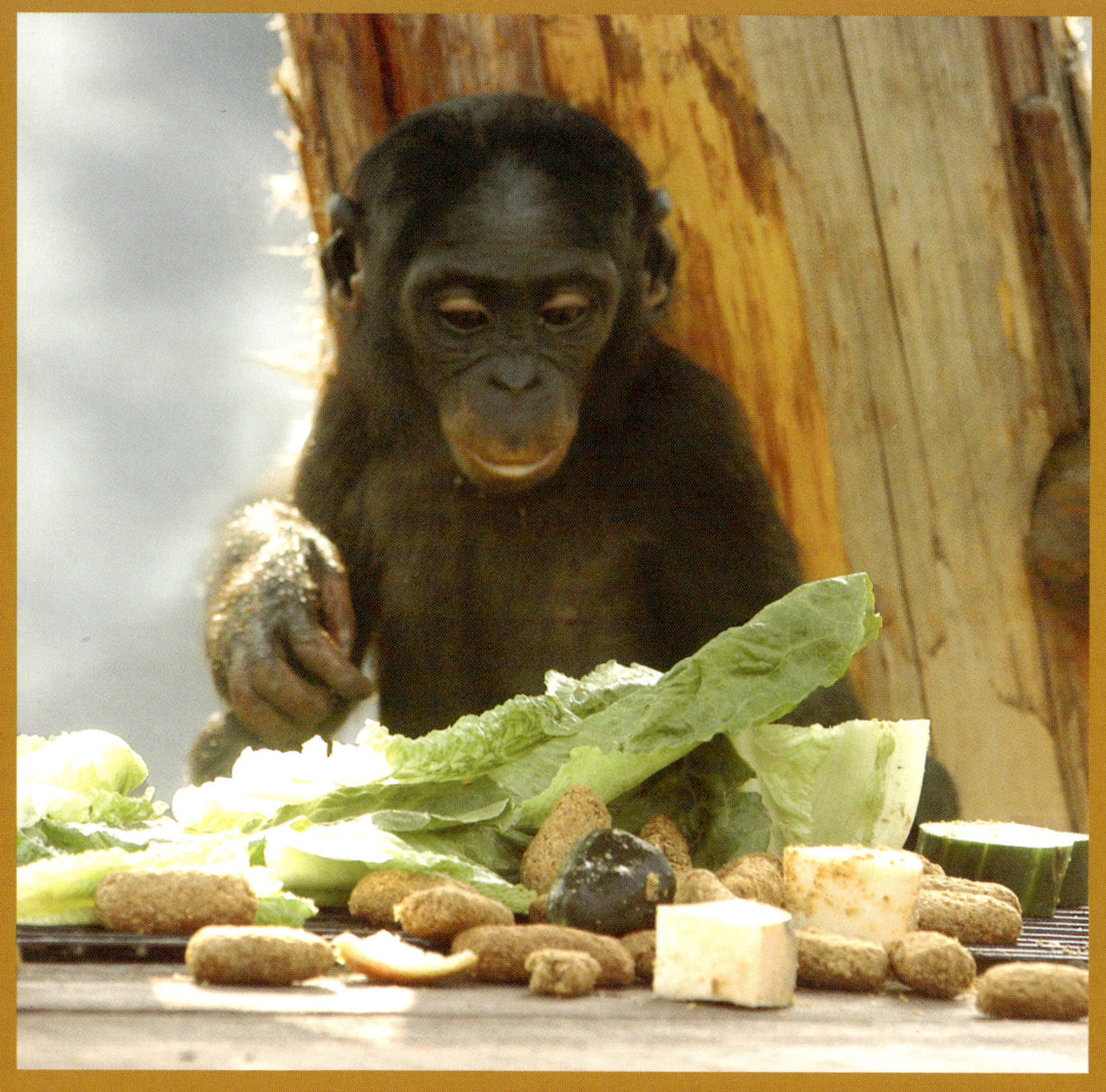

It's lunchtime! I love to eat my vegetables,
especially the cucumbers.
Those brown biscuits are supposed to be good for me,
but I think they taste yucky so I leave them for last.

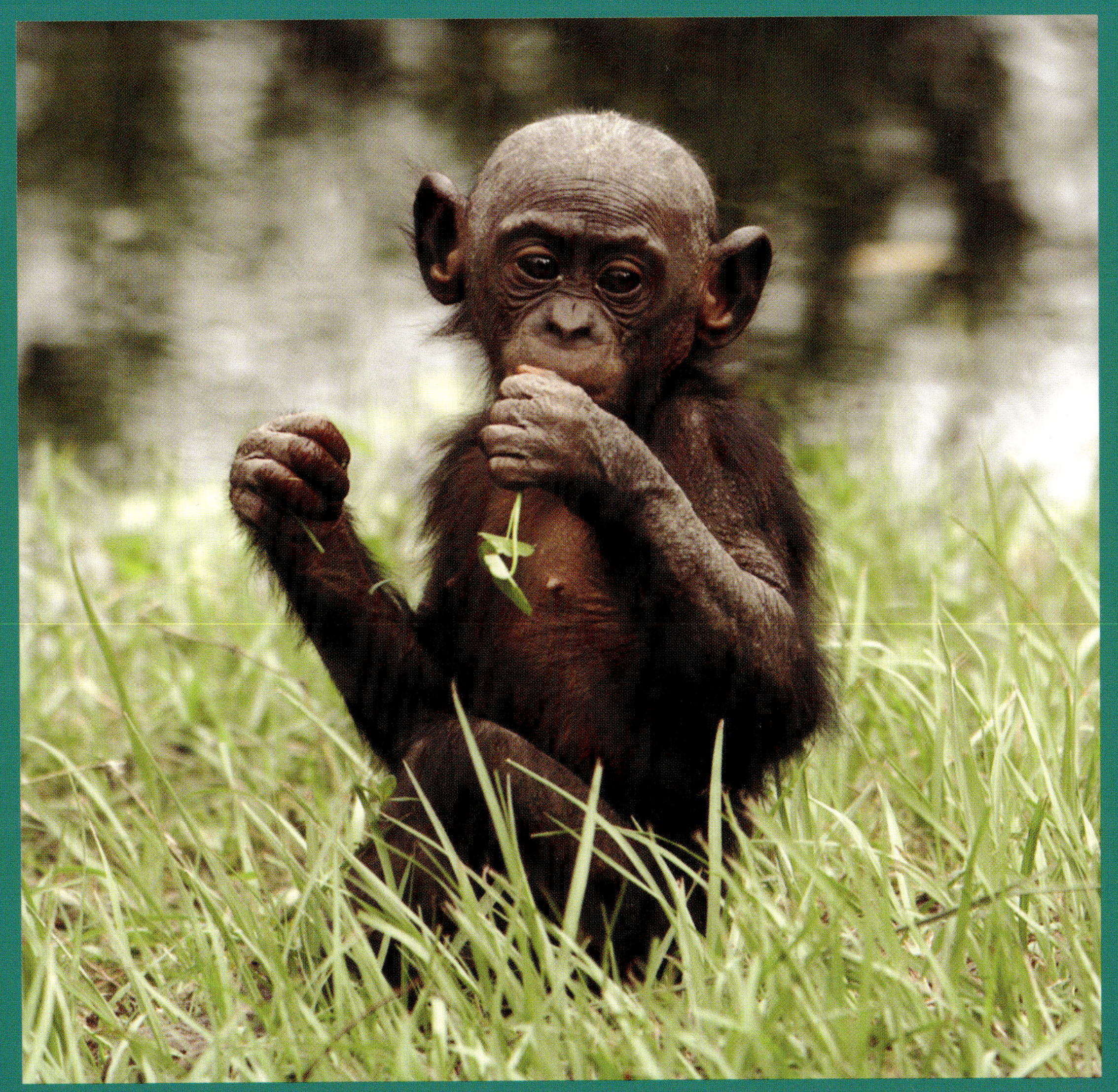

Kaleb likes to eat grass.

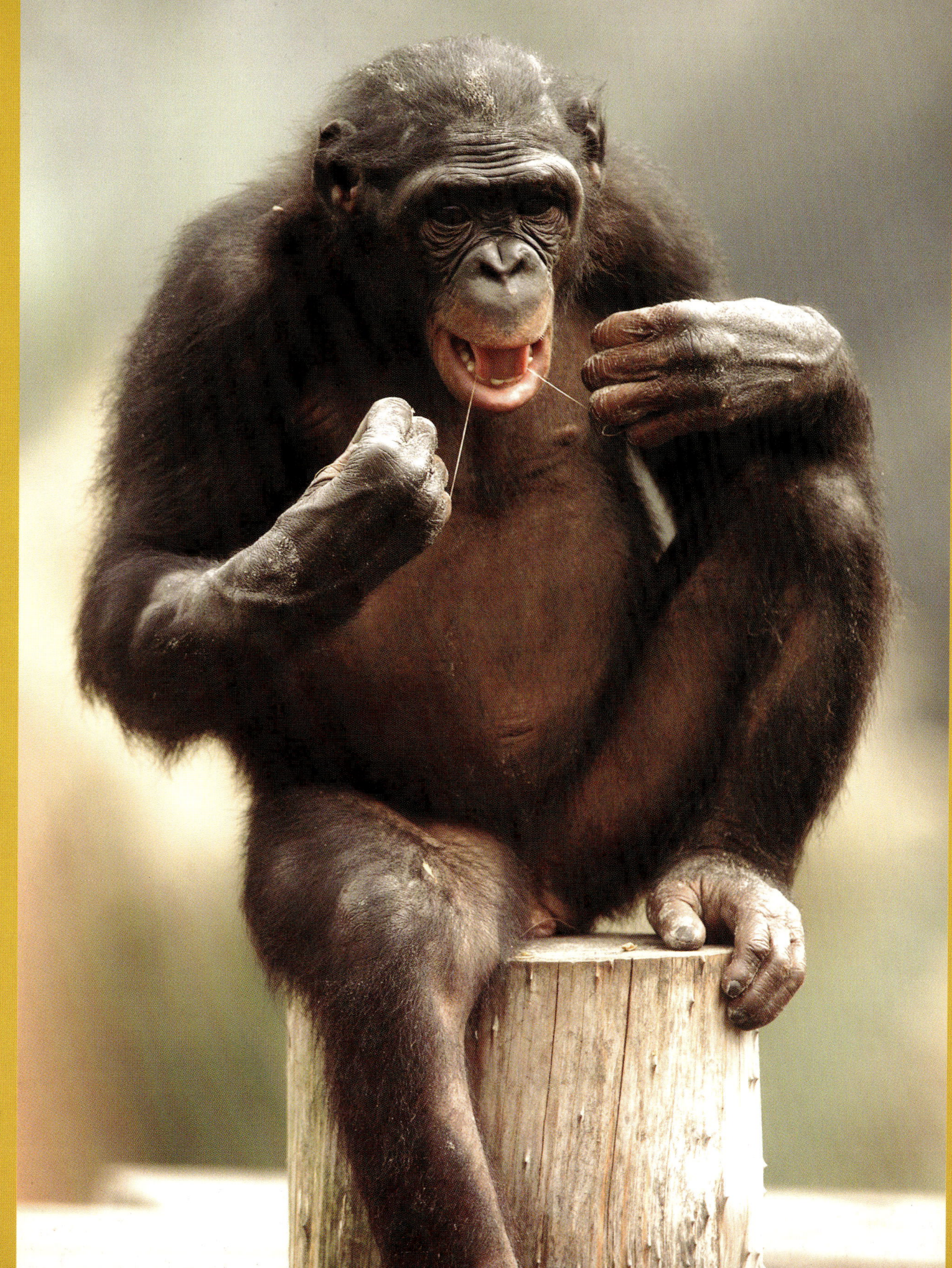

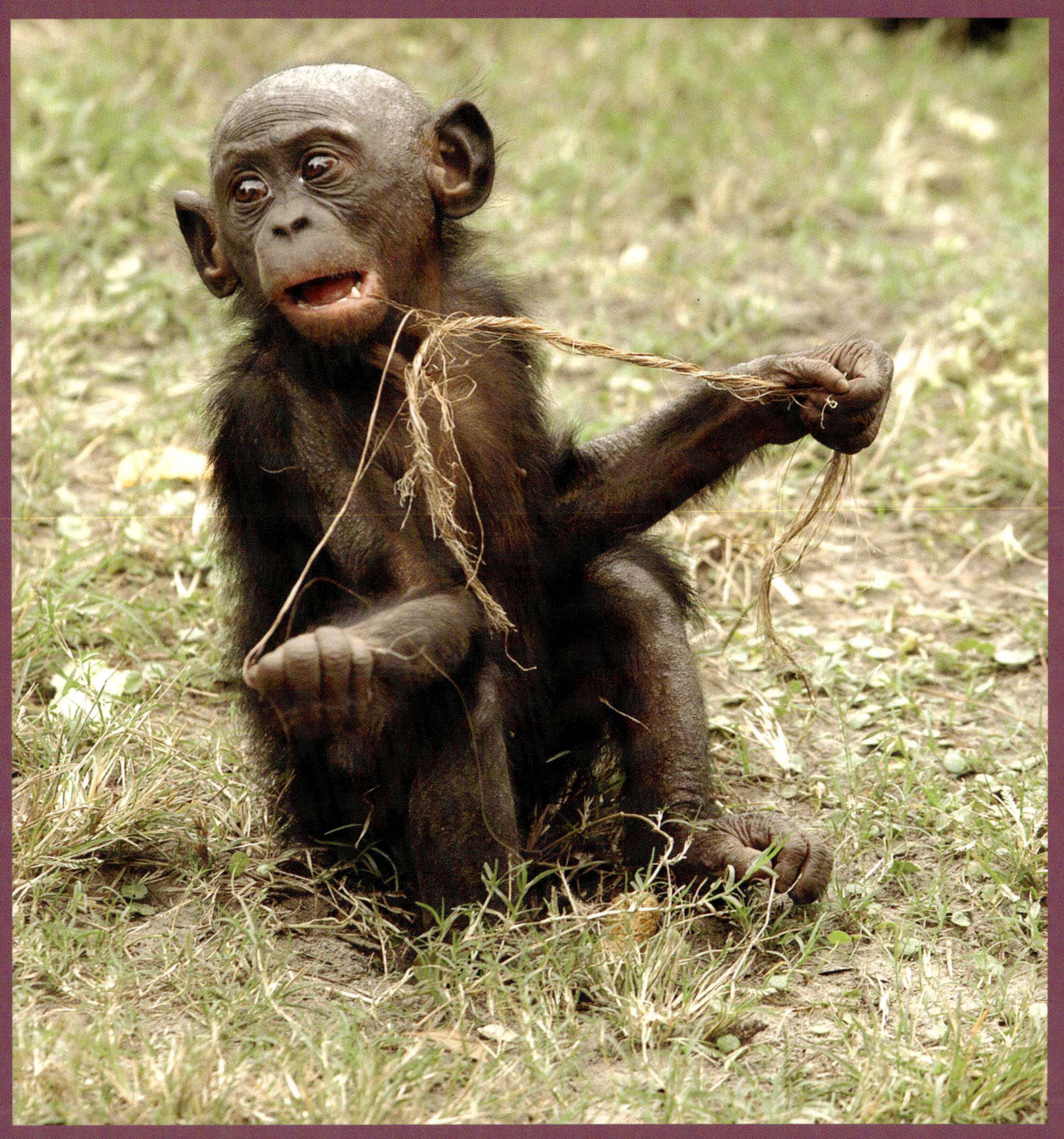

After lunch, he flosses with Aunt Lexi.

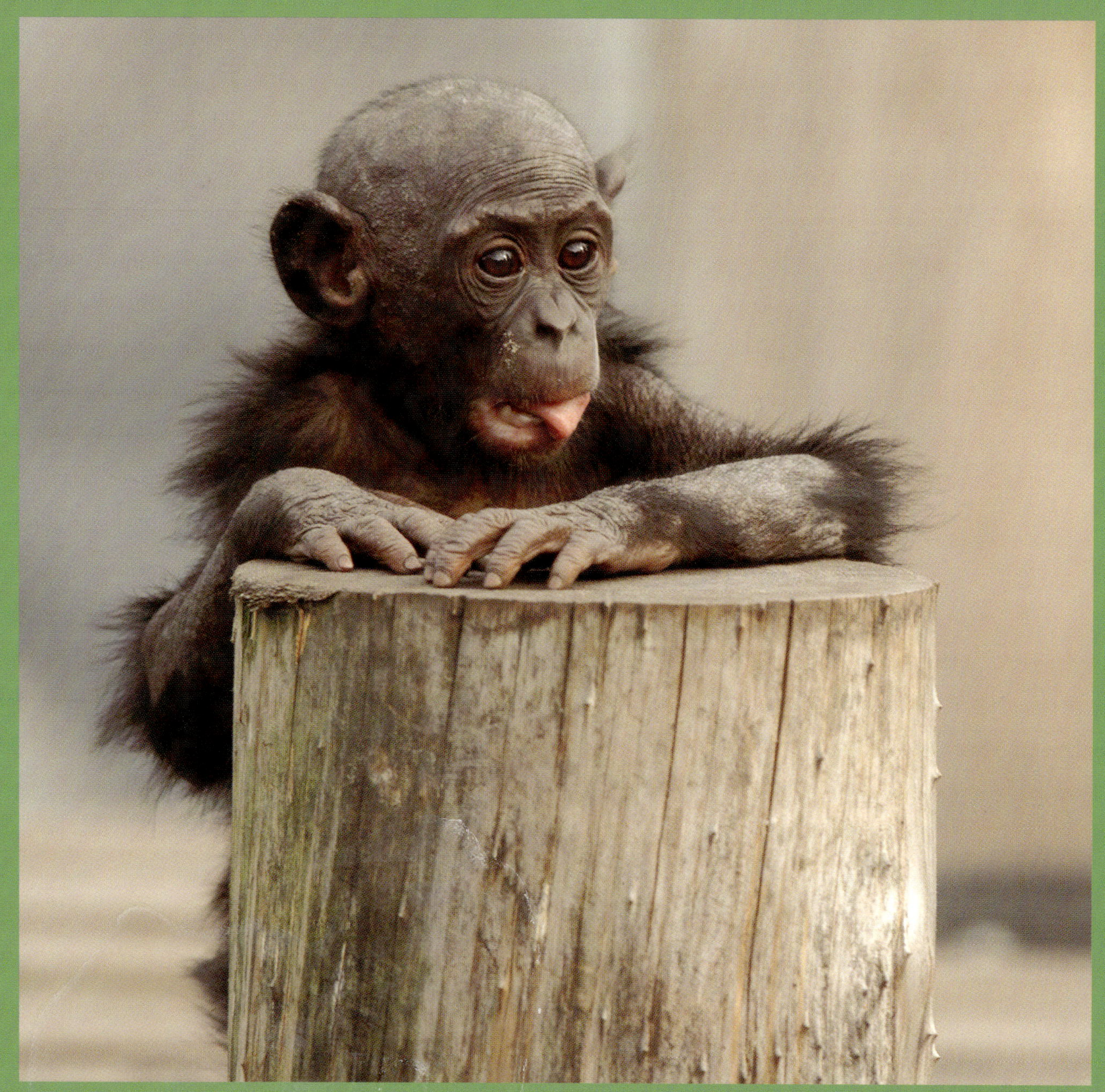

Sometimes Kaleb can get very silly.

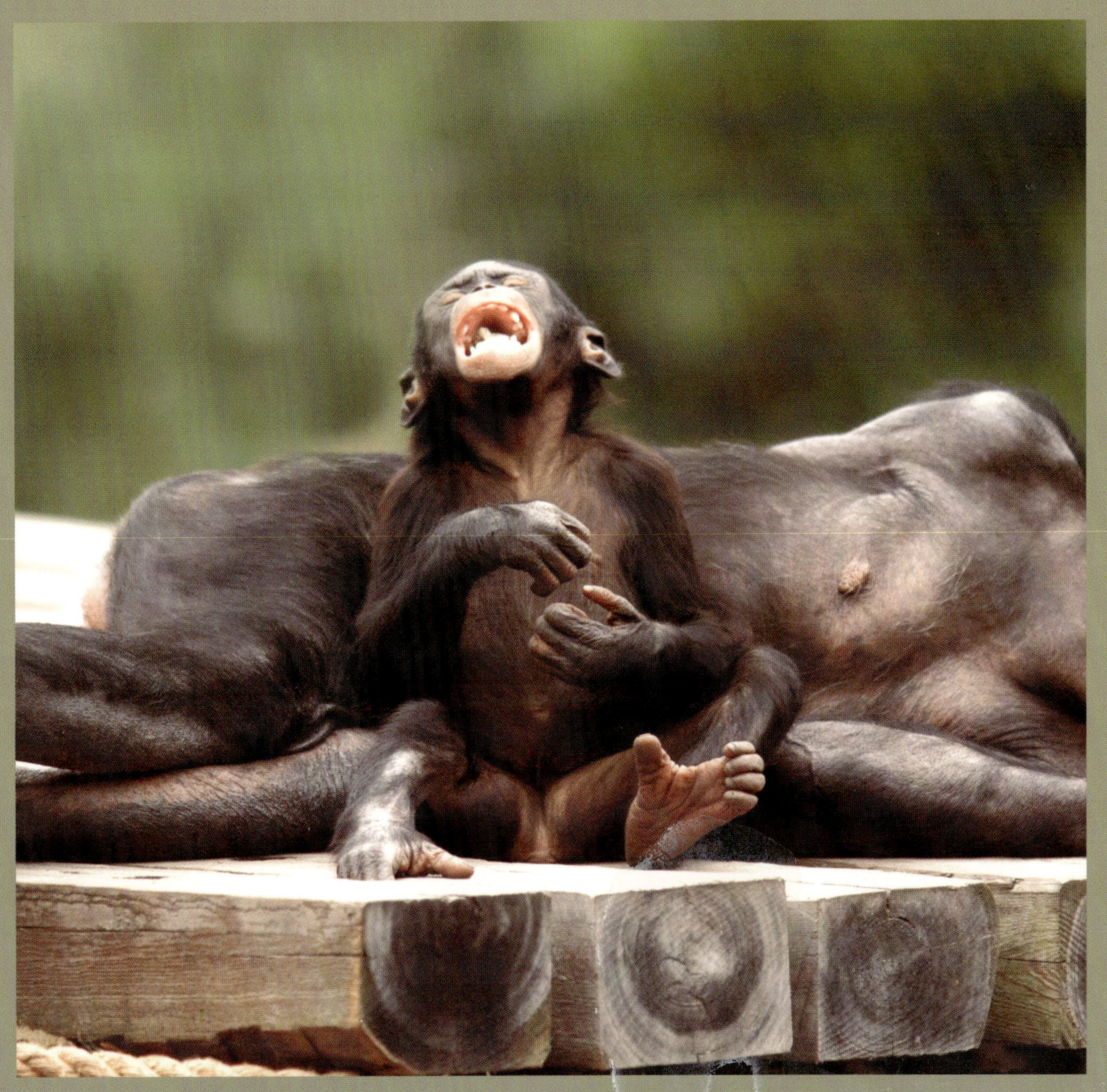

And this makes me laugh.

One time Kaleb climbed up on the roof even though he knew he wasn't supposed to.

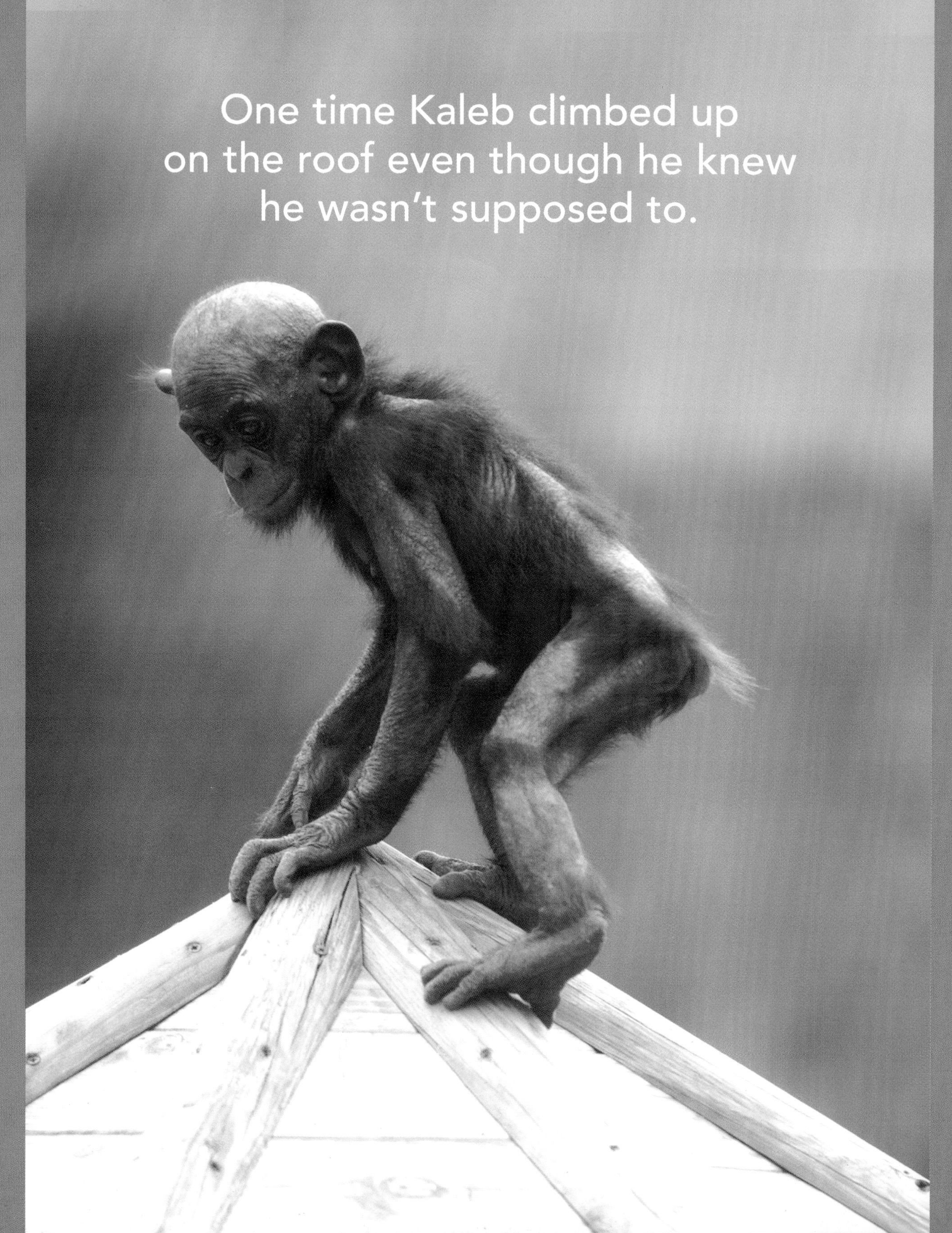

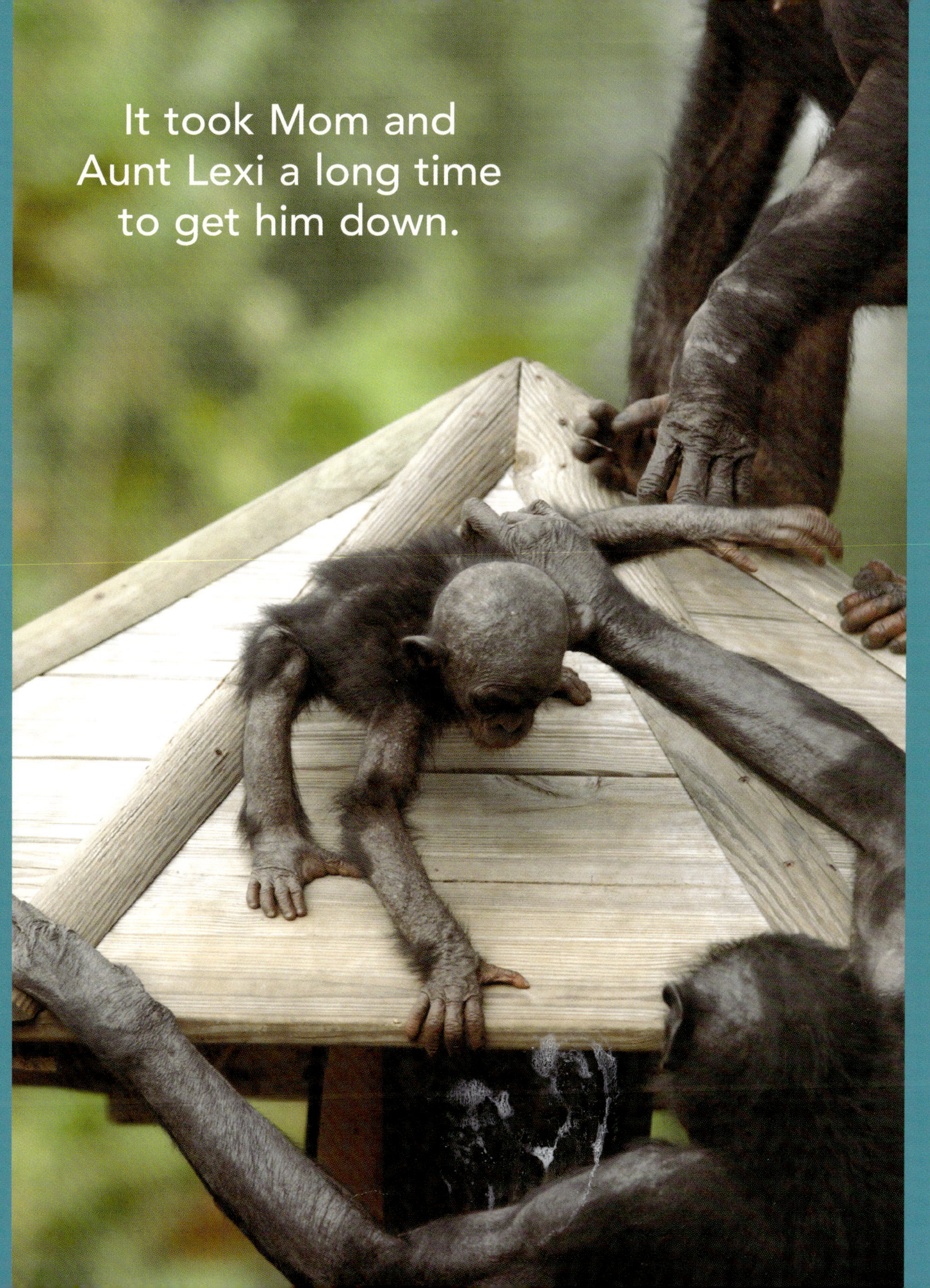

It took Mom and Aunt Lexi a long time to get him down.

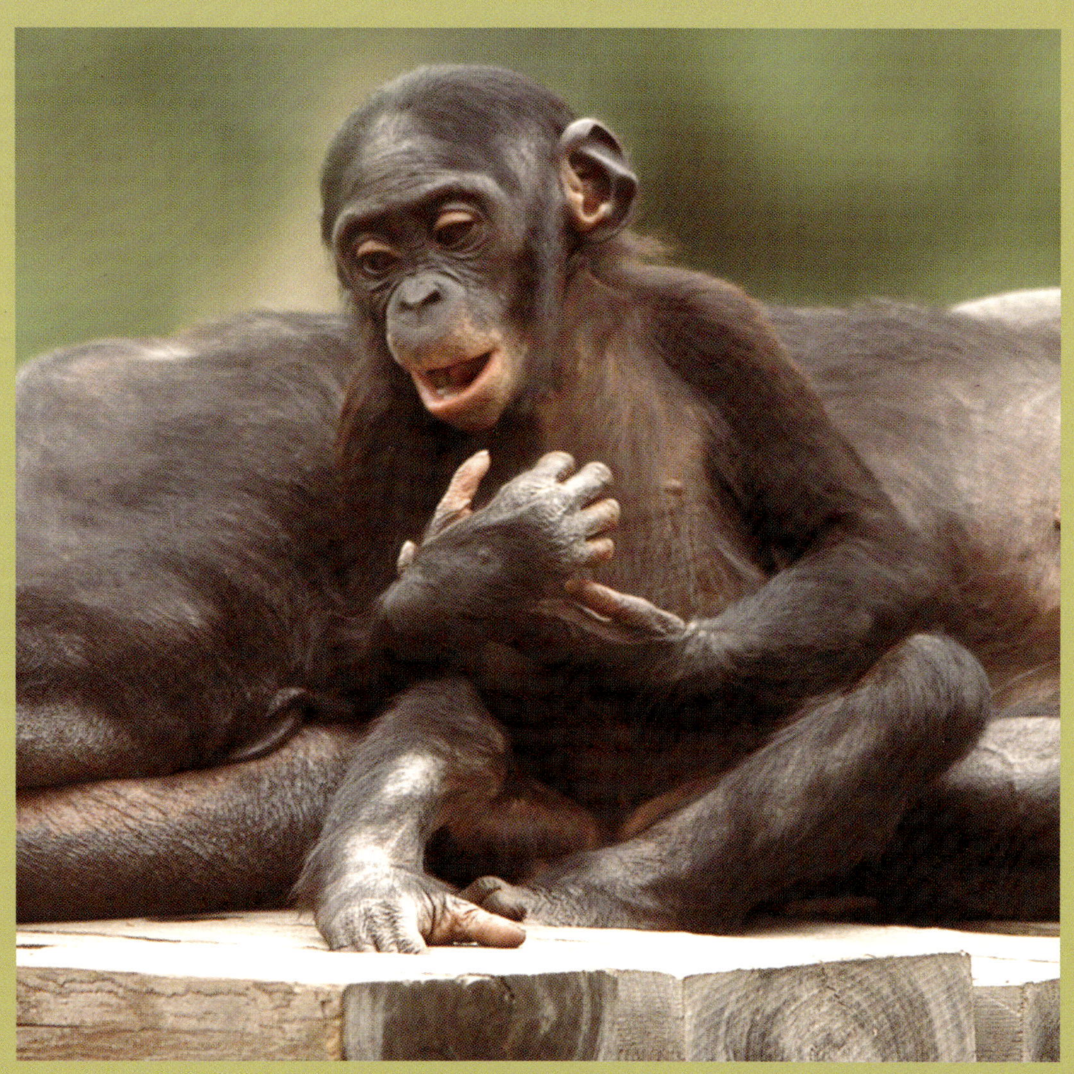

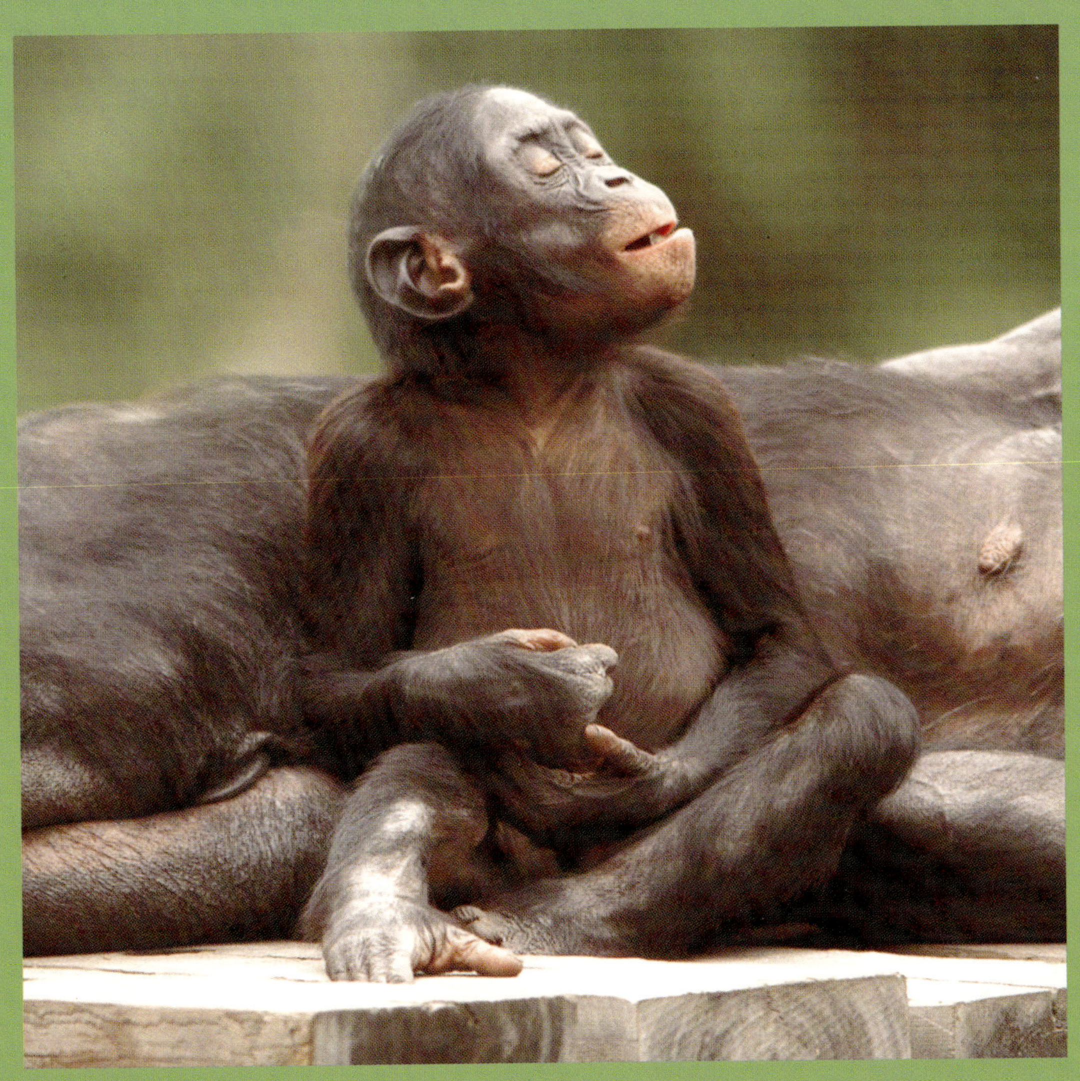

I'm a pretty good singer.

And Kaleb loves
to dance.

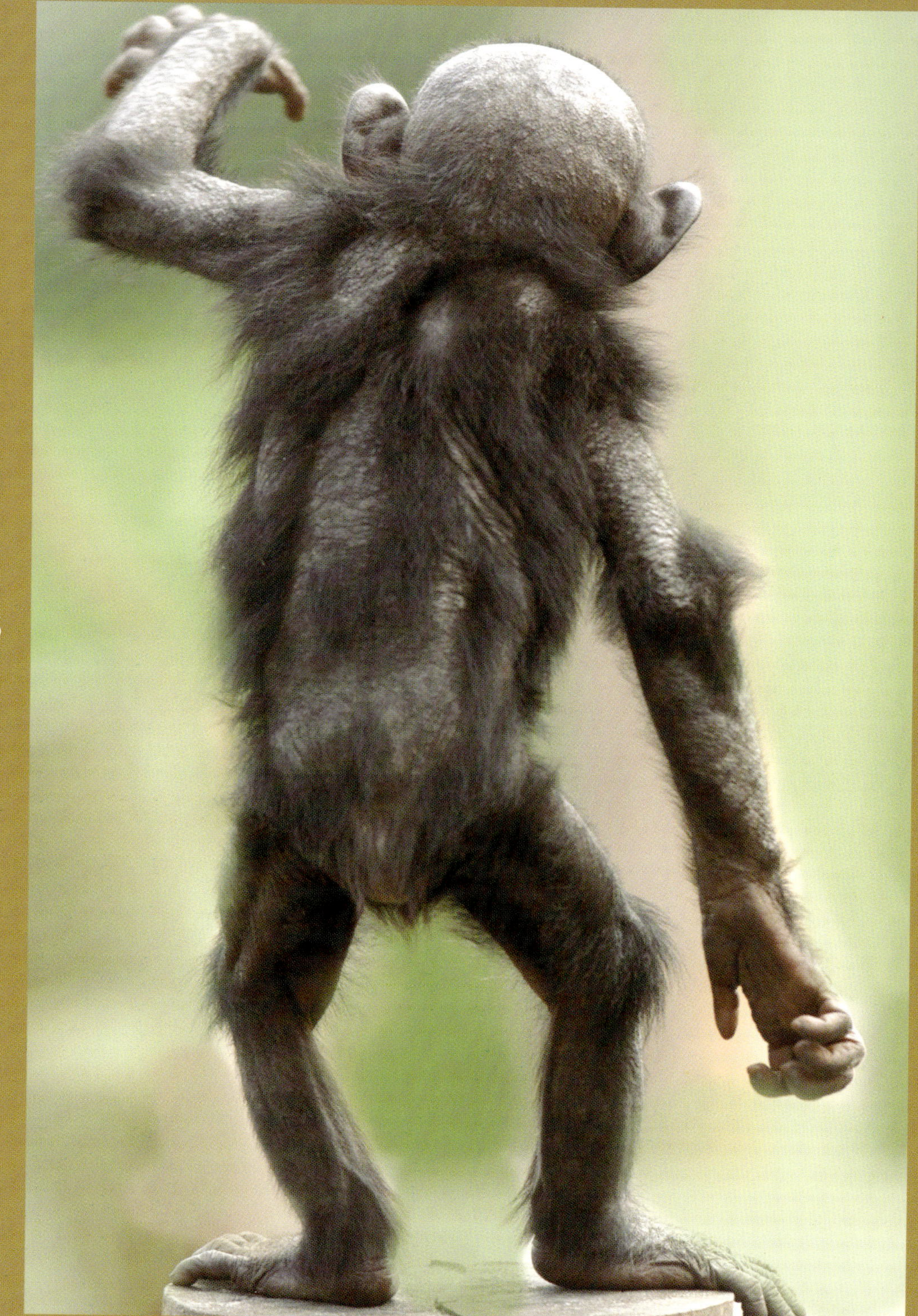

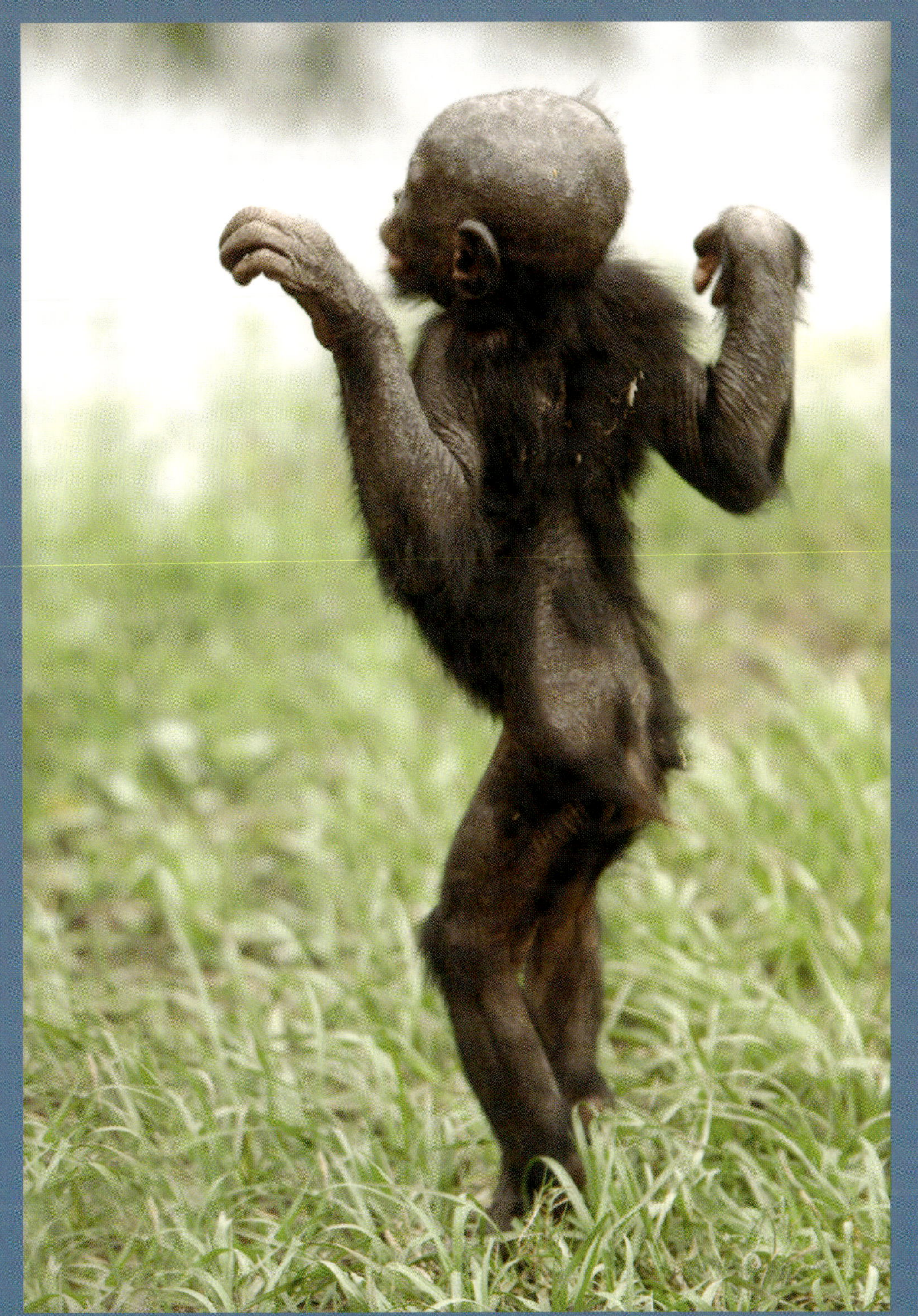

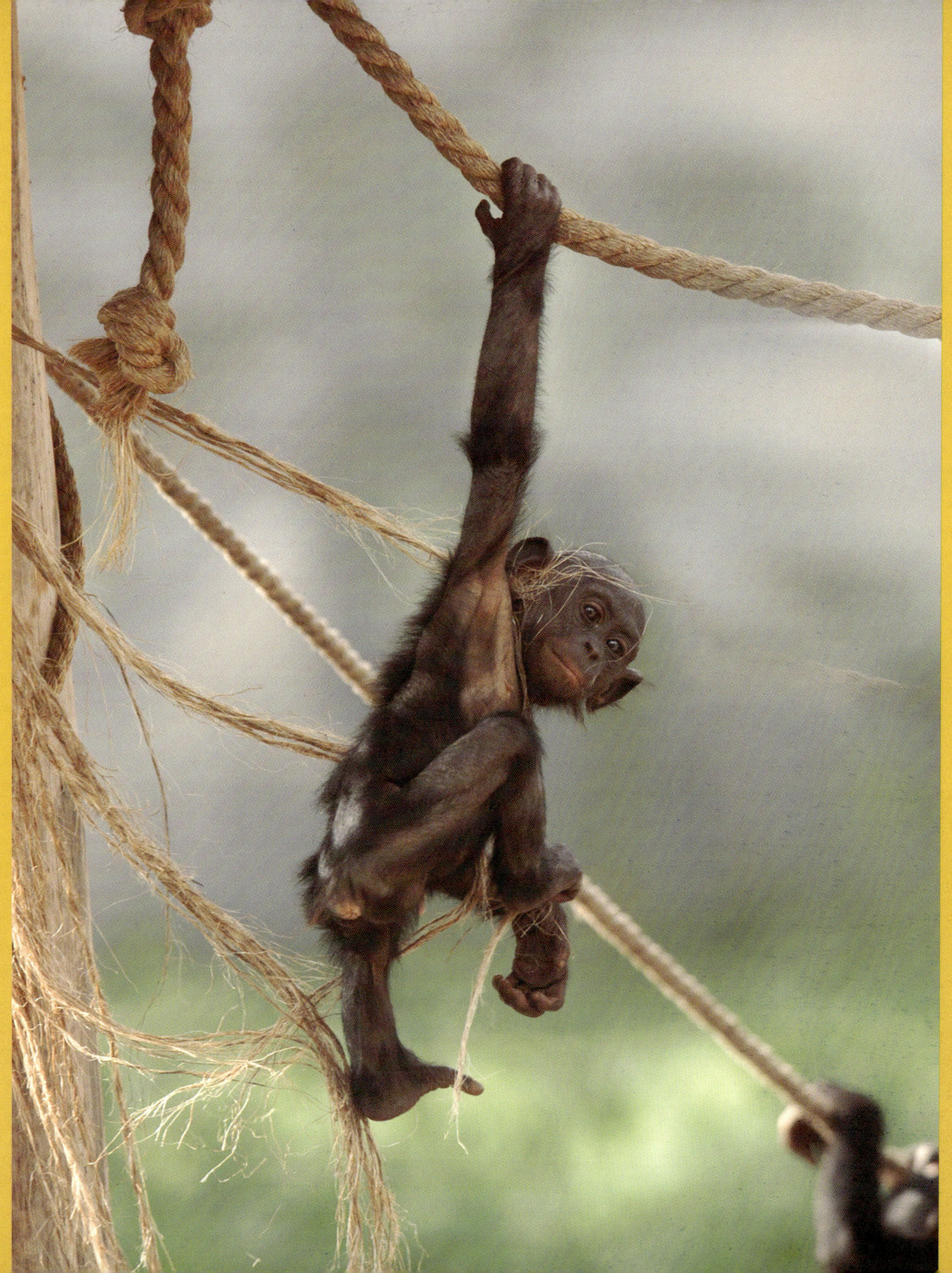

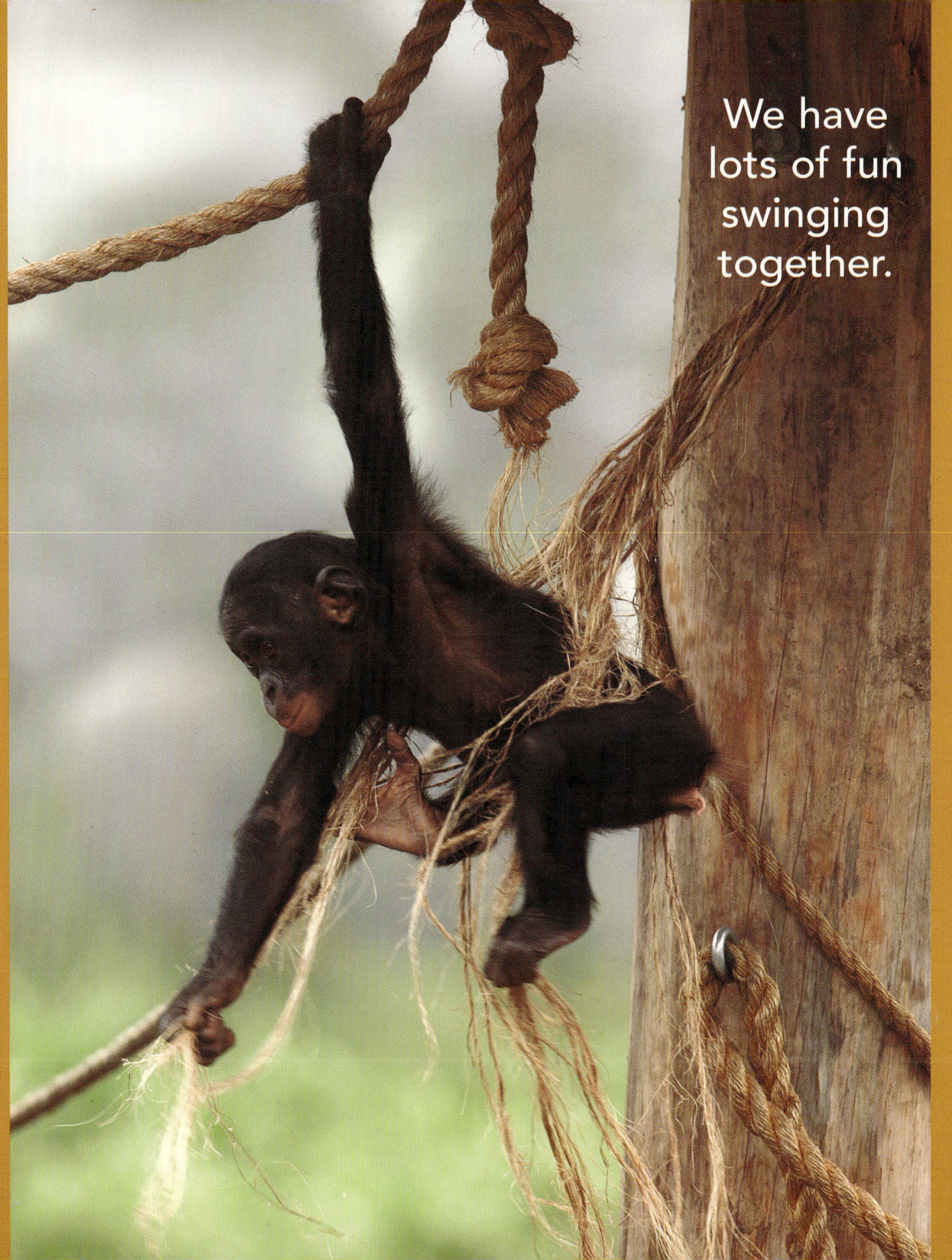

We have lots of fun swinging together.

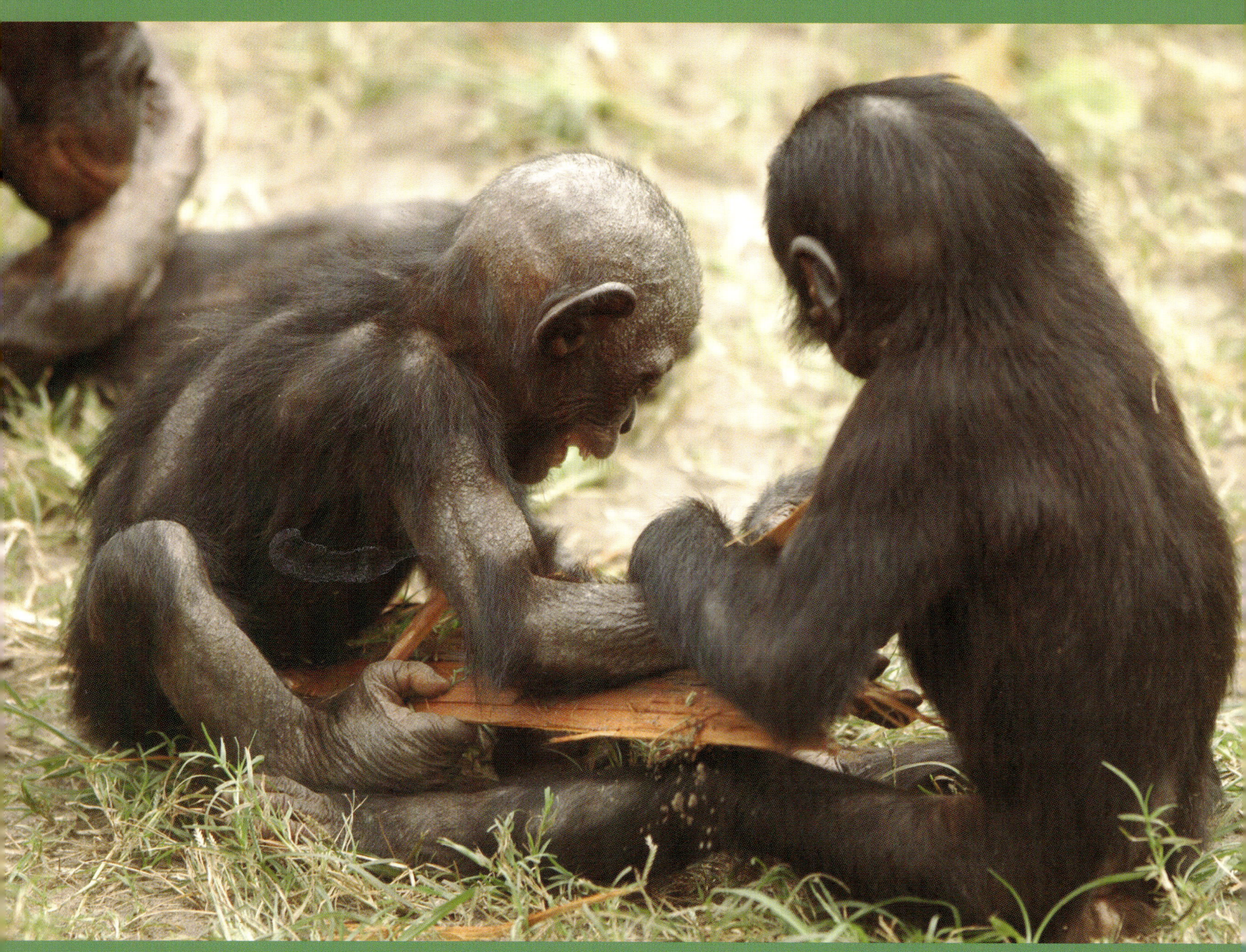

But sometimes we fight over the same toy.

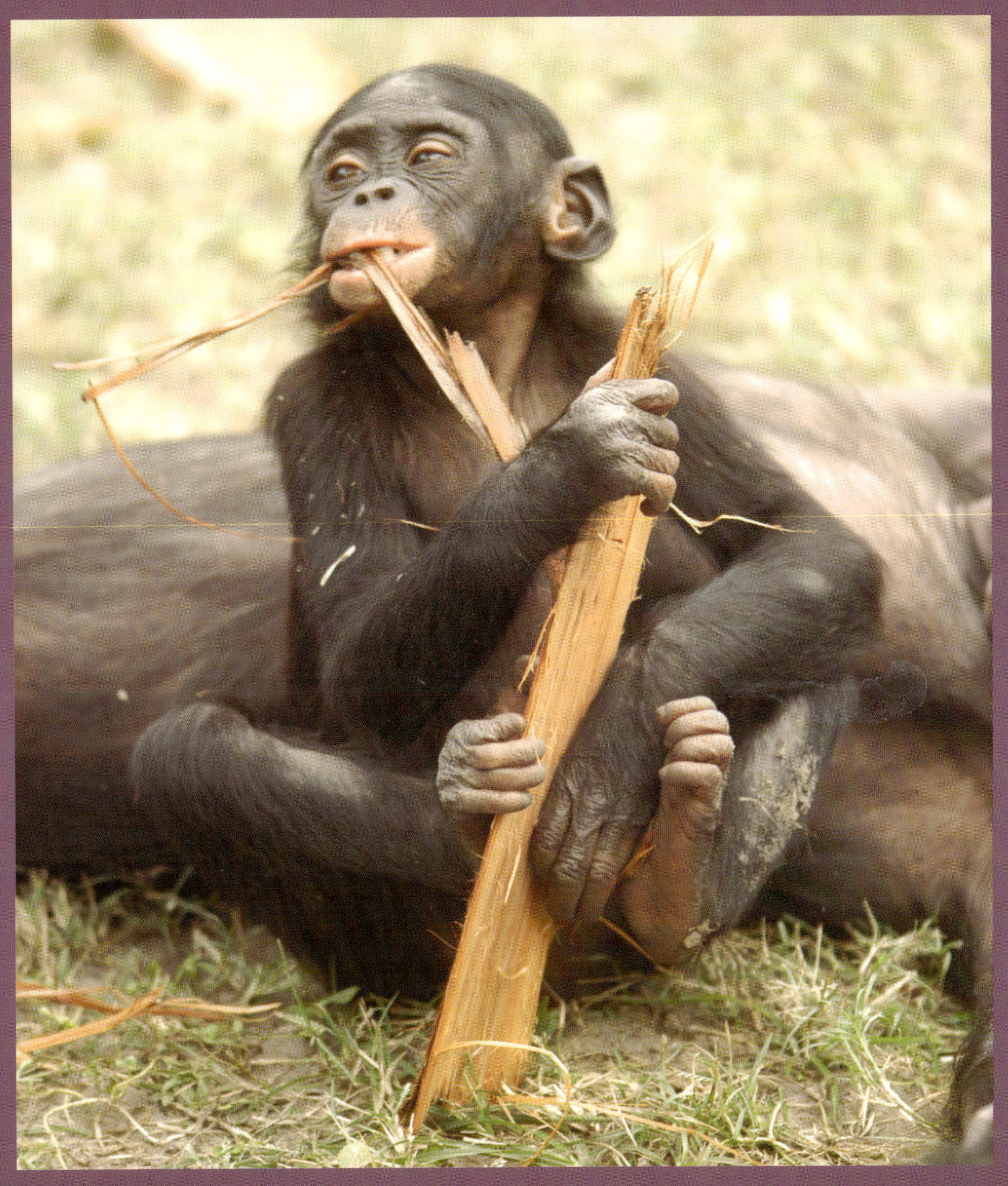

Today it's my turn.

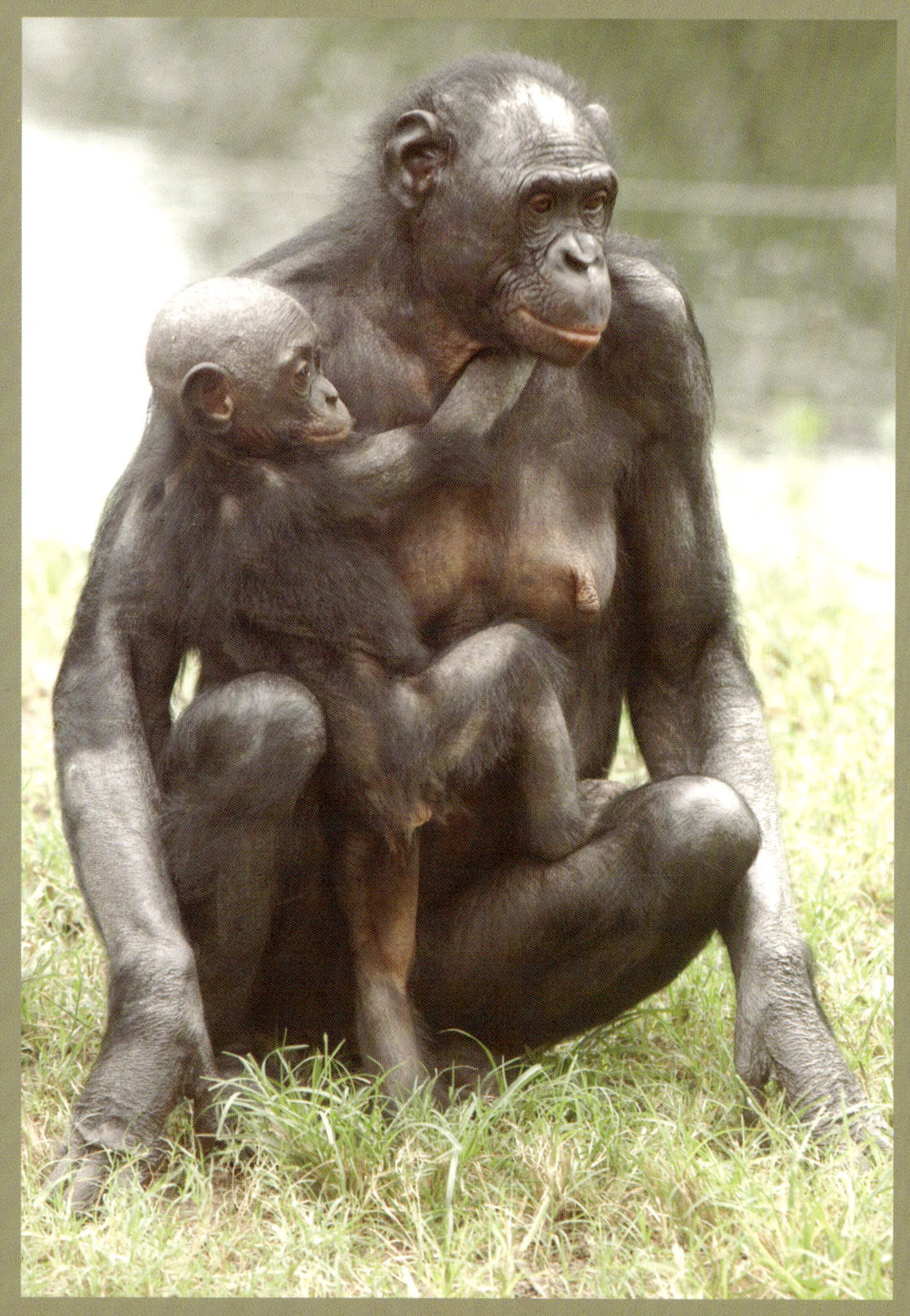

Most of all we love Mom time.

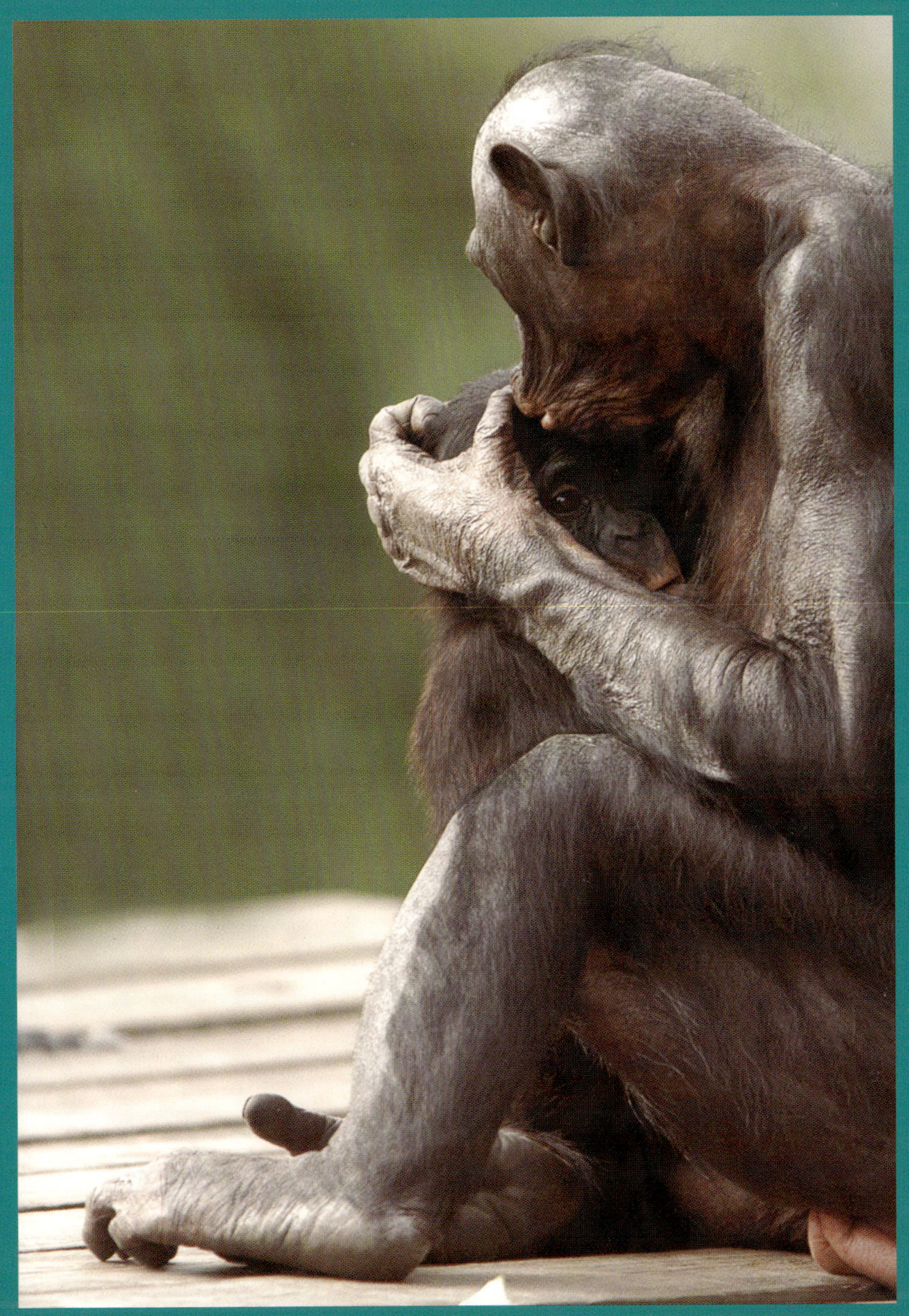

And big goodnight kisses.

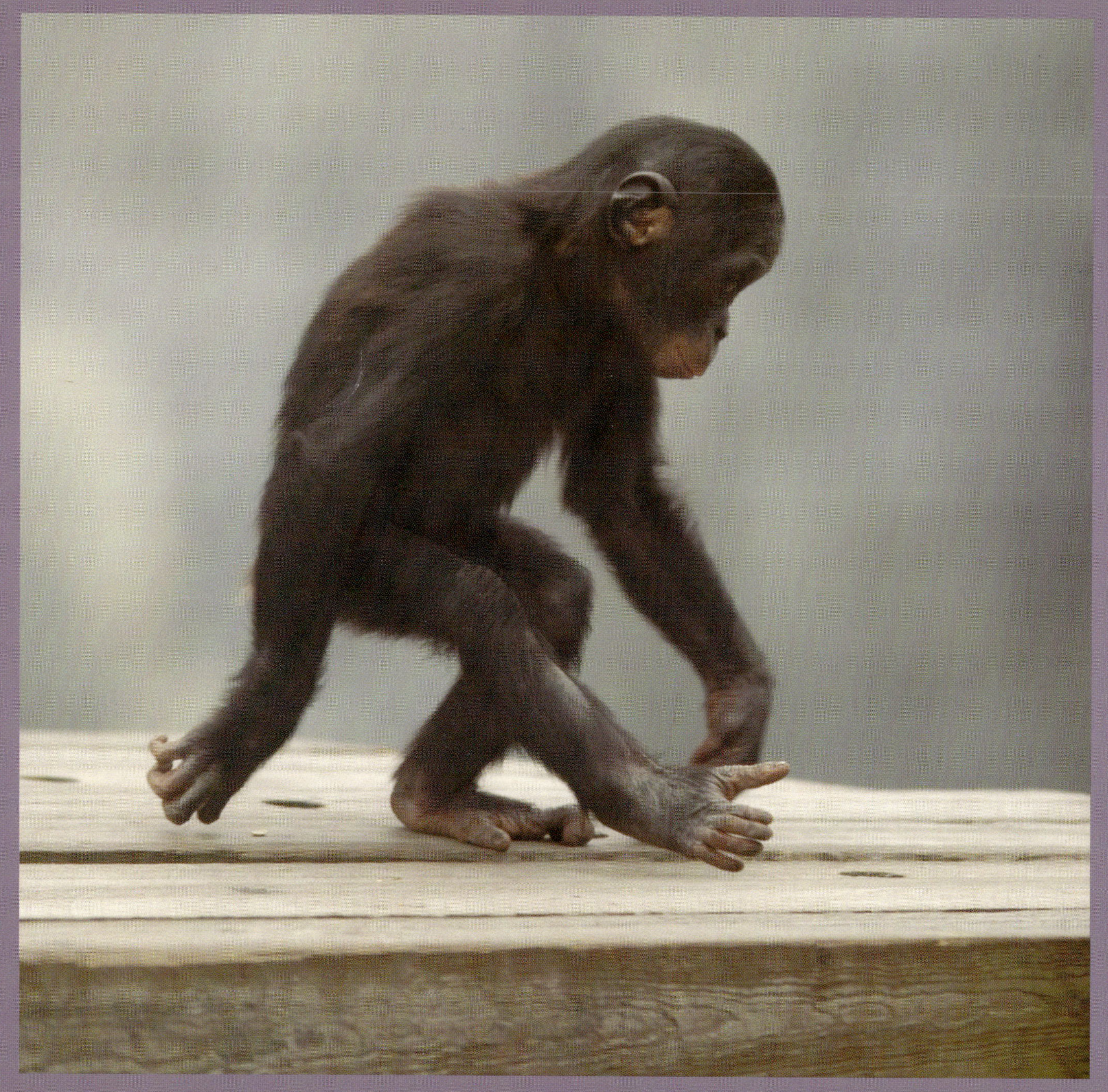

Now I'm off to bed. It's been a long day.
Goodnight. I hope you'll come see us soon.

Afterword for Parents by Jane Goodall

When I began my study of chimpanzees in 1960, bonobos were known as "pigmy chimpanzees". They live in the forests of the Congo Basin, south of the great Congo River, in the Democratic Republic of Congo (DRC). Eventually scientists began to study them in the wild and it became clear that they are quite different from chimpanzees: they look different, they certainly have very different calls, and their behavior is different too. They are more peaceful and the males and females are almost the same size. And so eventually it was decided to recognize them as a distinct species of great ape, along with chimpanzees, gorillas and orangutans.

Like chimpanzees, bonobos share about 99% of their DNA with humans (we are, in fact, a fifth species of great ape). More interesting for me is the fact that the structure of their brain is so like ours and they have intellectual abilities once thought unique to us: they can recognize themselves in mirrors, they have a sense of humor, and they show emotions similar to, perhaps the same as, those we call happiness, sadness, anger and so on. They communicate with many gestures that we also use, such as kissing, embracing, patting on the back, swaggering. And they express compassion and altruism in their society. They show, beyond doubt, that we are not the only beings on this planet with personalities, minds and, above all, feelings.

How sad that bonobos are in danger of becoming extinct, mainly through illegal hunting. I know some of the Japanese scientists who have been studying them for years. They had to stop because of the terrible civil war that ravaged the DRC for so long: When they went back, after the cease fire, two of their three study communities had been killed. No one knows how many bonobos are left in the wild — it may be fewer than 5,000.

Clearly, bonobos need our help if they are to survive in Africa. This is why I agreed to write an afterword to this enchanting book. The authors wisely use very few words, leaving the wonderful pictures to speak for themselves. The children — and surely many of their parents — who read *I'm Lucy* will be fascinated by this bonobo family, fall in love with Lucy and her brother Kaleb. And some will want to learn more, to know how they live in the magnificent rain forests of central Africa, how they find their food, how they interact with all the other creatures who inhabit that wild, far away world. And I believe that many readers will want to help us in our efforts to protect that world and to save the last of the bonobos and the other great apes, our closest living relatives, from extinction.

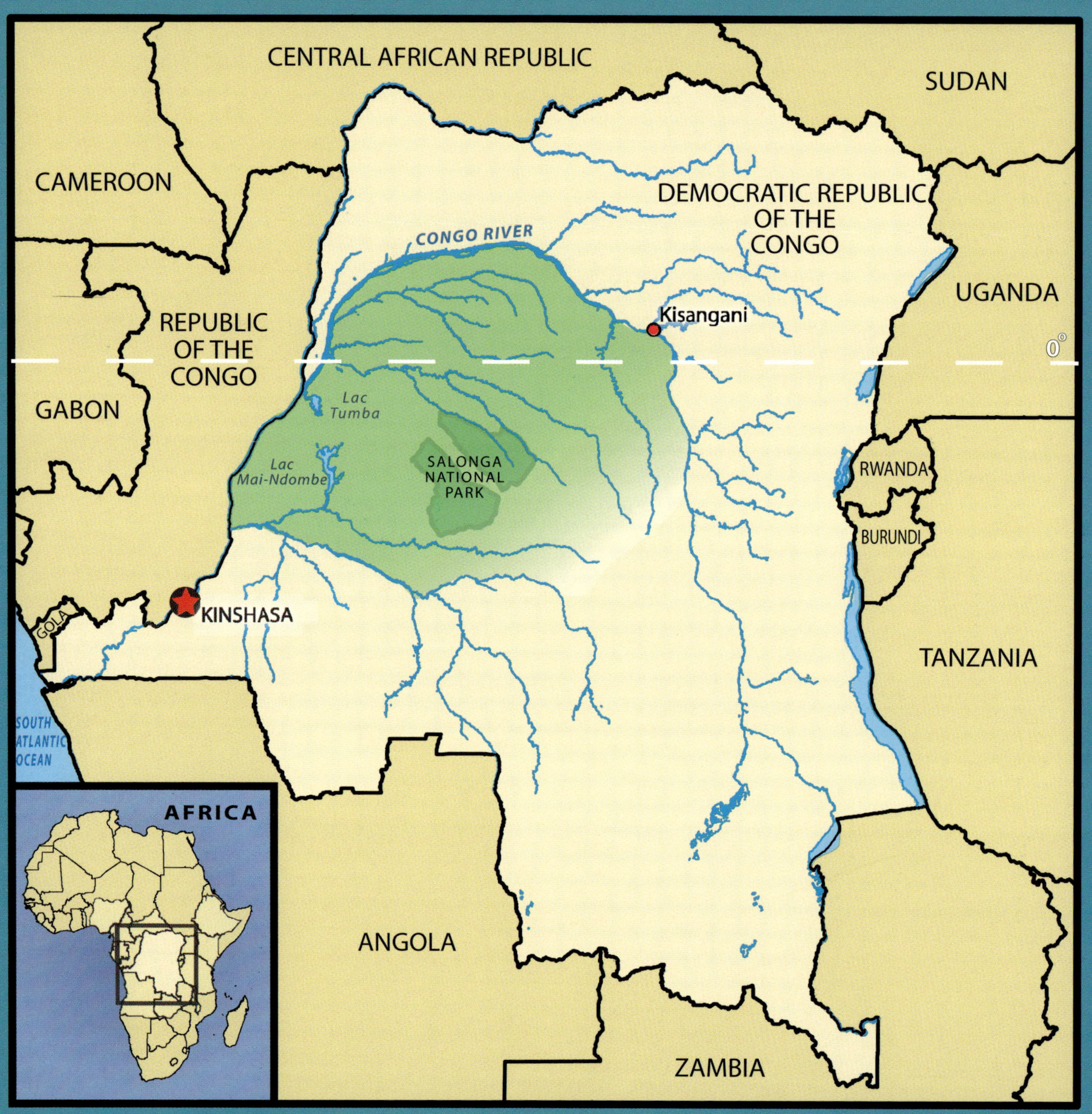

In the wild, bonobos live exclusively in the Democratic Republic of Congo, where their native habitat is shown in green on this map (created by Chris Auger for the Bonobo Conservation Initiative). You can learn more about bonobos, and find ways to help them, by visiting www.bonobokids.org.